Stumbling Over Eden

Steve Bonham

Stumbling Over Eden
Steve Bonham

Cover design and book design by
Steve Bonham and Christopher Lydon.

Published by Artisan Creative Ltd.
Derbyshire, UK.

www.artisan-creative.com

Printed by Amazon.

ISBN 978-1-9164548-6-6

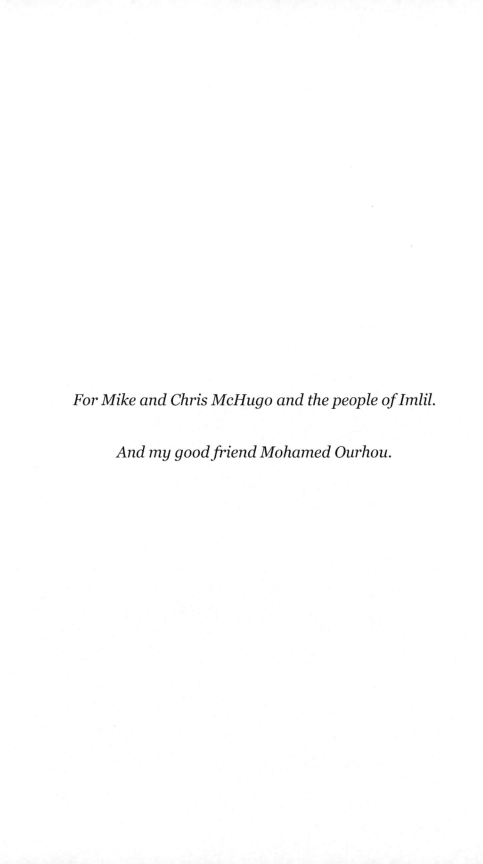

For Mike and Chris McHugo and the people of Imlil.

And my good friend Mohamed Ourhou.

Contents

Prologue

It started with a simple but probably crazy idea: to walk from the top of the Atlas Mountains into the Sahara Desert, a distance of 540 km. This is a tale of serendipity, exploration, self-discovery and freedom. My story involves the search for a lost tribe of dwarfs, discovering the lair of old warlords and an almost mythical Krupp cannon, travelling with a spirit dog and finding Eden. And much else.

It is the tale of my adventure, small, without unnecessary heroics but definitely mine. I offer it to you as evidence that the possibility of such is within us all. I am no hardened warrior of the road. This is a tale for the adventurous at heart.

What makes an adventure? The word has its roots in the Latin *adventurus*, capturing the state of sensing something is about to happen without knowing what; a sense something emerging from the unknown, bubbling up in the alchemical soup of the concealed in the mystifying. It is this uncertainty and unpredictability that are the raw materials of adventure.

More or less any human activity can be done adventurously if we embrace the wondrous improbability of the passing moment, and this is the attraction of putting on your walking boots and setting off. You are moving at a pace where things can come to you.

Of course, we can avoid uncertainty by not venturing towards it or we can try to plan it out of existence. But that would take away the chance and delight of it. An adventure happens when you embrace the unexpected about where you are, where you are going, who you meet, what will happen next. Adventures don't have to be dangerous, but it can help.

To embark on an adventure puts you in the flow of the unfolding world, and this is the way of the vagabond. To be a vagabond is an ancient calling; it is to move across the earth unbound by expectation or control. It is to adopt the clear but compassionate gaze of the outsider. Being a vagabond also has the piquancy of being subversive. Our betters do not like us to move and see for ourselves.

The 1824 Vagrancy Act stipulates that 'every person wandering abroad and lodging in any barn or outhouse, or in any deserted or unoccupied building, or in the open air or under a tent, or in any cart or wagon ... shall be deemed a rogue and a vagabond.'

And why Morocco? I have been coming to Morocco for more than twenty years, since I first travelled to the Atlas Mountains and discovered a people and a place that enchanted me. Morocco is a liminal place in so many ways. It is the borderlands for so many things. The borderlands between peoples; between the continents of Africa and Europe; between religious traditions, Judaism, Islam and Christianity and probably the echoes of the pagan; between ideas of freedom and possession; between the revealed and the unrevealed; between the lost and found. It is by its very nature an adventurous place.

And so I set off with my companion Moha and two mules and their owners Hassan and Muhammad and this is the tale I was given to tell. On the road, the world becomes personal and singular. This is not a travelogue *per se*, nor a particularly detailed account of the geography or history of a region. But all these things are woven within it.

The vagabond way is to let what happens, happen, accept it and travel on. And this is what I have tried to capture in the opening out and unfolding of the adventure. There are probably too many mentions of eating and drinking (or not eating and drinking) but that was the way it was. And such obsessions are not that rare for a footsore traveller! Sometimes the narrative may take a digression or two as a chance thought captured my imagination and I sailed away with it. And sometimes I have glossed over a section or two of the trip where the road became monotonous and time offered nothing to remember.

I walked this road five years ago. My deep appreciation goes out to those who helped me tell it today. They include: for love, support, enthusiasm (and careful reading) Orla Flynn; for the care and attention to the manuscript, my old friend Peter Harvey; for the technical wizardry of preparing this book and uploading it, Chris 'the Bishop' Lydon. And to the people who bought advance copies and encouraged me to press on with this.

And to Mohamed Ourhou, guide extraordinaire and brother of the road.

Thank you, thank you, thank you.

Map

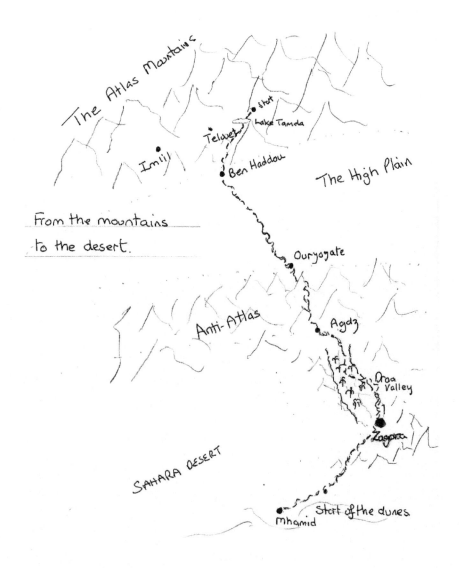

Chapter 1: On Top of the World

Over ten years ago I found myself on top of Mount Toubkal, the highest point in North Africa. I stood there under a battered tin sign that marks the top. To the north runs the Atlas ridge that takes you to Europe, a place from which – since time immemorial – ideas, blood and power have flown back and forward. To the south lies the rest of Africa, different and complex, and most immediately Mauritania, a desert land in which slavery is still real and evident[1]. To the west is the Maghreb (in Arabic 'the place of the setting sun'), once the edge of the world and the start of the dreaming of what lay beyond. And to the east, the Sahara.

Ah, the Sahara. It has always entranced me. From my childhood reading of the stories of Lawrence of Arabia to travelling in it with the explorer and writer Robert Twigger, and finding in the sands the flint arrow heads of a fishing people who once sat on the banks of a great lake, its mystery and magic have echoed in my imagination.

I could not help but look east from the top of this magnificent mountain over the snows to what lay beyond. And in my mind's eye I imagined the long caravans of camels snaking out of the shimmering heat from the southeast, from mysterious places like Timbuktu. And reflect that before them would rise the huge ranges of the Anti-Atlas and the Atlas Mountains which, weary and worn from the desert, they would have to climb to get to the rich trading cities like Marrakech and Fez on the other side.

---

[1] Notwithstanding that the evil of it snakes its way all over the world.

Perhaps it was the lack of oxygen that made me fanciful. As I sat there looking out over the High Atlas range through air as clear as the day it was made, the notion that I might travel over these ancient, time-shattered peaks all the way to the start of the desert surfaced in my mind. And as it did so, I cursed ruefully, as it was immediately obvious that it was one of those ideas that must be nurtured and adapted to, like an unplanned child. To walk from this 'highest spot' on and over into the great, sprawling wilderness of the Sahara Desert was an offer from the gods which I could not turn down.

But it was nearly ten years later that the heavens aligned and the call became irresistible.

One of the things that has kept me going over the years is that a great idea and the action that must follow do not have to be contiguous – that it is okay to wait for an idea to swell and grow, like a seed well planted. Of course, there is a danger here of procrastination and I have without doubt been guilty of that; but part of the art of life surely is to recognise the right moment, when through time, rain and sun the seed is ripe for harvesting. And it was in May 2017 that the time was right.

To the inevitable question from others – why? – I should say that at that point I didn't really have a clear idea.

I have noticed this before: that a compelling idea at the right time seems to attract a richness of unforeseen opportunities to it - a kind of cosmic serendipity where a single seed becomes a bigger harvest.

I knew my destination had to be the dunes of the desert itself. The sands of the Sahara only make up about 20 percent of the 9.2 million square kilometres of the whole of the desert. But it is the sands that resonate and move. Curving across the planet like great slow-motion waves, at dawn and dusk they are some of the loveliest sights you can see. They can bury peoples and places. People such as the Garamantes. These were farmers, engineers and merchants who lived and thrived from 500BC to 500AD in the northern Sahara. They built a city not based on rivers but on irrigation systems and wells till the water dried up and the sands overwhelmed them. Then there is the maybe mythical city of Ubar, the 'Atlantis of the Sands', where people traded the bitter perfume of frankincense until God swallowed up the place for offending Him.

I found someone who nearly did make the trip - Gavin Maxwell. Gavin Maxwell was one of those spell makers who cast magic over my childhood with his wonderful book *Ring of Bright Water*. For several years, I nursed a resulting ambition to live on an island on the West Coast of Scotland looking after otters. Oh, and following the film of it, with someone who looked a lot like Virginia McKenna.

Much later when I first went to Morocco, I came across another book by Maxwell called *Lords of The Atlas*. It is about an astonishing period of Moroccan history which played out in the area through which I would trek. As the book cover says, it 'tells the extraordinary story of the Madani and Thami el Glaoui, warlord brothers who carved out a feudal fiefdom in southern Morocco in the early twentieth century. Quislings of the French colonial administration, they combined the aggression of gangland mobsters with the opulence of hereditary Indian princes and ruled with a mixture of flamboyance and terror. On returning from the coronation of Queen Elizabeth II in 1953, Thami ordered the severed heads of his enemies to be mounted on his gates.'

This astonishing story captures the imagination of anyone who would read it, seemingly set like something straight out of medieval history and so current its witnesses might still be alive. And at the heart of the story is a Krupp cannon which I imagined I might find.

Featuring stunning photographs by Maxwell himself, the writing is beautifully wrought and evocative. I would travel through many of the places mentioned in the book, some of which he would not have visited himself. As a Scottish aristocrat, he got access to palaces, old papers, pashas and princes, and cars to drive him around, but his time there was limited to the sort of stuff hidden from us common folk. But it may be that I was also undertaking a journey he had planned but never made. Shortly before leaving, I picked a second-hand copy of the biography of the author by Donald Botting, who knew Maxwell well both as a friend and a fellow explorer. In it he describes how Maxwell was desperate to do an expedition on foot and mule and for Botting to join him. He wrote a letter to his friend imploring him to come.

"We MUST do the trip and nothing must stand in the way, you'd agree if you had seen the mountains and the mountain's Kasbahs – it's a country that it's impossible to exaggerate pictorially."[2]

---

[2] *Gavin Maxwell: A Life*, Douglas Botting, HarperCollins, 1993.

It appears the trip never happened - probably beset by the money and personal problems that dogged Gavin Maxwell through his life, it seems to have been shelved.

And then there was the issue of the tribe, or indeed tribes, of dwarfs.

My old friend the writer Robert Twigger – he of my trips to the desert – had first mentioned the rumours when he heard I was going. Recounting a tale which he had heard from his friend Tahir Shah, he said to me:

"I always meant to go there – to look for the 'The Lost Tribe of Dwarfs' which are rumoured to live somewhere in the more remote parts of the other side of the Atlas."

Now Rob is prone to come out with these statements. His brain is an attic room of old maps, documents, discarded laboratory equipment, rumours, and rocking horses. Sometimes when you ask him 'tell me more', he can be vague and a bit mysterious, as if he has revealed something that perhaps you should not hear.

So, I hit the internet and after a while revealed a series of archive documents concerning dwarfs in the remote region around the Draa valley through which I would be rambling. I ordered a reprint of these, which arrived some weeks later titled: *The Dwarfs of Mount Atlas: The Collected Papers on the Curious Anthropology of Robert Grant Halliburton.*

These, it turns out, were serious arguments at the end of the 19th Century put forward by a Canadian lawyer, Robert Halliburton, for the existence, on the south-eastern side of the Atlas Mountains, of a tribe of curly-haired, red-skinned dwarfs. Not surprisingly, this was a somewhat controversial assertion, with vigorous debates in various academic bodies. The papers have the petulantly defiant tone of someone who writes suspecting people are sniggering behind his back.

In one of the papers, he describes a people from Akka 'no higher than four feet (1.22m), a peculiar reddish colour... who wore red leather boots or leggings coming up nearly to the knee and their knife or dagger has a peculiar crescent-shaped handle. They made spindles and other small articles, which they sold at markets." He also said they were "very brave and active."[3]

Halliburton continued to insist that he had more than enough evidence to prove this true until the day he died. After which the controversy seems to have died away.

Many of the places in the papers are hard to trace, but Akka exists. It is a small town near the Algerian border and the other places seemed to stretch east of here into the region through which I would be travelling. So perhaps ...

The region itself was almost unvisited by westerners – indeed the reason the French armed the Gluoui with modern weapons was to keep this remote area under some sort of control. It could just be that a people who were neither Berber nor Arab also lived here at one time. Halliburton wondered if they were related to the pygmies of Central Africa. Could these have moved north at one time in distant

---

[3] *The Dwarfs of Mount Atlas*, Coachwhip Publications, Landisville, 2009.

history? Morocco has, I have found, a way of revealing its secrets very, very slowly.

But the greatest, most compelling reason for this adventure was this: having travelled to the Atlas Mountains many times, I have developed not just a love for the Berber people but also for what they represent. They give the lie to the idea of kingdoms and kings; they are a timeless people spread across North Africa, a people who include the Tuareg, whose idea of society has proved resilient beyond belief as successive despots have tried to squash and eradicate their unique character. I had trekked many times in the Atlas Mountains and each time had come away feeling enriched by what I had discovered.

So it was in the middle of 2016 that I took up the idea again as I sensed parts of my life slowing and closing, and towards the end of autumn made a firm commitment. The following March I flew over to see my old friend Abdu at the Kasbah di Toubkal in Imlil, Morocco to talk to him about the practicalities. He is an ex-trekking guide and fixer of all things within the arcane ways of Berber societies. He had found me a Berber guide, Moha, who was mad enough to attempt the trek. The three of us met up sitting round a table on the roof of the Kasbah drinking mint tea and trying to make sense of things with a variety of maps.

As far as they knew, no one had attempted this before and, as there was no planned route, Abdu was a vague as to how far it would be.

"Stiv, I think this could be 450 – 550 km may be more."

Moha nodded.

Given my hard-learned understanding that Berbers underestimate time and distance when talking to westerners, I reckoned that would be 300 miles or more, and the estimate proved ultimately to be pretty accurate.

We agreed that I would walk the old-fashioned way, on foot with mules and then camels carrying supplies from the highest pass over the Atlas Mountains across a high plateau and then over the Anti-Atlas Mountains to the Draa Valley and on to a small military town called M'hamid near the Algerian border. We would follow broadly the old camel routes but when these became circuitous or followed long stretches of modern tarmacadam roads, we would take a more direct route.

Between us we reckoned it would take around three weeks. About one hundred miles a week, five days at a time with two rest days. We were going to set off at the start of May, which is towards the end of the trekking season when the weather is starting to get really hot. Abdu was worried about the heat on the final section into the desert, but reckoned it would still be cold, even frosty, up in the mountains.

I headed back to England to get ready. Over the previous months of the winter, I had been trying get fit. I had walked regularly with my old chum Tim up in the Derbyshire Peaks where I lived, did my 10,000 steps every day for my Fitbit but I knew that was not enough. Now I am not one of those hardened, scrawny types who start salivating at the idea of beasting themselves through uncompromising wildernesses wearing as little as possible. I am a slightly overweight guy with a dodgy knee who has been known to experience the odd moment of self-pity. It has been one of the enigmas of my life that someone lacking the necessary design credentials is so drawn to doing extreme things. Anyway, the thought of twenty miles plus a day through a remote and rugged region of deserts and mountains was enough of a prompt to send me twice a week to a climbing wall inside a church in Derby. I was not anticipating I would be climbing any difficult ascents but I did want to increase my sure-footedness, core stability and ease of travel.

The good people there found me an instructor called Rob who was a slight and spry guy training to be a stuntman. He would arrive at the sessions having just injured himself fire-eating, fencing, crashing cars or indulging in some similar life-threatening activity.

On our first day together, he watched me climb up a route.

I got to the top quite quickly and felt rather proud of myself.

"You climb like a typical bloke," he said contemptuously. "Thinking you're just gonna haul yourself up with your arms because you can! Climbing is problem solving and physics – come down here."

And with references to those well-known mountaineers Pythagoras, Euclid, and Sir Isaac Newton, he introduced me to the idea of using my own weight as an aid not an obstacle to my ascent. I had to climb up walls using only my legs for upward propulsion, I was not allowed to raise my arms much above shoulder height, I had to try on occasions to get myself horizontal to the ground about three metres above it. For days after, I would walk around like a saddle-sore cowboy muttering to myself:

"Bruising occurs when one forgets that to every action there is an equal and opposite reaction ..."

But it did me good physically. With these lessons, all the above exercise and regular Pilates, I probably left England fitter and stronger than I had ever been. I also learned another thing from Rob which I still carry with me: when faced with a challenge, stand back and think more widely about how you are going to approach it – don't get bogged down with what you think you see. There is always another way up!

Chapter 2: The Road to Telouet

I woke up in one of the rooms of the Kasbah du Toubkal which hangs somewhere between the village of Imlil and the towering presence of the highest mountains in North Africa. Outside, a cock crowed and somewhere across the valley I heard the Muezzin call the valley to prayers. Light streamed in through the cracks in the rough wooden blinds and I could hear the joshing and shoving of the Kasbah staff, mainly young Berber men from the village below. On a forgotten breeze, I could smell the ghosts of the woodfires and mint tea that would greet my nostrils many years ago when I first came to this place. These days the woodfires have more or less gone but the memory remains. The government encourages the use of the camping-gas stoves to stop the erosion of the tree stock that lies between the pockets of pasture and garden in the valley bottoms and the sharp, snow-covered faces of the mountain peaks that rise magnificent and monumental all around.

If ever I would think of a sanctuary in my life, it would be here. I had arrived late the previous night, walking up the steep winding path which ran under the walnut trees up to the big wooden doors of the Kasbah. The journey here had been more eventful than usual: an unexpected violent storm had broken out over Marrakech and the plane had to abort the landing and return to Casablanca until it had passed. I hoped it wasn't an omen.

All journeys in Morocco start for me at the Kasbah du Toubkal. I have been coming here since the turn of the millennium. Back then there was only a broken dirt road after a long and somewhat perilous drive up from Azni and intermittent electricity. The Kasbah and its founder Mike McHugo, his brother Chris and Haj Maurice have been a catalyst for much change for the good in the area since repairing the Kasbah and opening it as an idiosyncratic and completely of itself Berber refuge cum hotel. Profits have in part gone towards promoting projects that have brought health and education resources to the community.

Dragging myself into the day, my first job after washing and dressing was to re-sort and pack all my stuff. I was determined on this trip to be an efficient traveller. Usually, I am not. I was also determined to get up and start at my own pace. I was still haunted by the horrors of getting up in the dark in a tent in Ontario with it -35° outside and instantly starting to pack my toboggan, dismantling tents, trying to eat breakfast and preparing to leave before or as it got light. Some people are built for rapid starts in the dark, but I am not one of them. The impact is usually a day of chaos and uncertainty about what I have forgotten, where I have put things, and the grim anticipation of repeating the nightmare the following morning.

So, with this in mind I established a strict routine for myself to getting up and getting ready, which I promised to adhere to every day of the trip. This included each piece in the same place every day and if finding I had forgotten to pack something in the right place being prepared to open up my rucksacks or carry bag and not just stuff it into a corner, but make sure it was returned to its allotted space.

So it was after a good breakfast, some decent coffee and well-wishes from Abdul and his friends that I set off back down the hillside into the village of Imlil to drive the apparently short distance to Telouet and start the expedition from there.

Telouet is home to the grotesque remains of the kasbah of the Lords of the Atlas, the fearsome but compelling Glaoui clan. I had decided I didn't need to start at the top of Mount Toubkal itself, having already summited a few years ago and not wanting to eat into the time I had available. Anyway, this fulcrum for the strange story of the Glaoui was more than high and redolent enough to be the perfect embarcation point for my adventure.

The story of the rise of Glaoui begins up here in the high passes of the Atlas Mountains and involves a dying sultan and a famous cannon. Morocco has never been an easy place to rule and rulers, Moroccan rulers, generation after generation, were forced to go on a regular progress (known as a harka) around their country settling disputes, quelling uprisings, executing malcontents in extreme and creative ways, and generally making sure a large boot was kept firmly on the neck of the population.

This progress was a logistical nightmare in which a whole army and royal court would decamp in the morning, packing up huge number of tents, marquees and temporary shelters, march for a few hours before stopping to rebuild the whole camp again. Alongside thousands of soldiers, there would be tent erectors, musicians, dancing girls, cooks, servants, courtiers, religious officials, government bureaucrats, snake charmers and acrobats and people to look after the horses.

Sultan Moulay Hassan set off on one such progress in 1893. He was determined to show his face to his truculent subjects and also to visit the great oasis from which his family had originally come – Tafilelt.

From the start it was a disaster. The court was always short of food and even for Morocco it was unreasonably hot. It was nearly winter when he reached Tafilelt. And then he had to head back lest trouble should start to brew on the other side of the mountains.

To get back to Marrakesh and cross the formidable High Atlas Mountains there are three main routes.

Nearest to the desert to the south was the pass, Tiz'n'Test, controlled by the M'Tougga tribe; more centrally there was the Oued Nifis; and lastly, furthest north, was the Tizi'n'Tishka controlled by the Glaoui under the leadership of Madani El Glaoui and his brother, Thami. Tizi'n'Tishka back then ran through the stronghold of the brothers at Telouet.

All three tribes made their living by being state-endorsed gangsters demanding payment in kind or gold from the caravans of dates, argan oil, walnuts and other goods that arrived from Timbuktu and the deserts to the south. Those who refused to pay were quickly and painfully put to death and their goods confiscated.

This was a kind of surrogate protection money to which the Sultan turned a blind eye in the hope that it would keep the tribes happy, occupied and well behaved. In fact, he made the leaders of each of these tribes 'Caids' – his official representatives in the region. This pseudo-legitimacy in fact only encouraged their ambition. The Glaoui had also another sort of wealth to boost their sense of destiny in the existence of salt mines around their territory.

In choosing to cross the High Atlas via Telouet, Sultan Boulay Hassan was making one of those decisions the consequences of which would ripple on for centuries. Even to the point of making it my destination that day.

He set off as winter broke hard upon the mountains. His followers were in a terrible condition. Thousands died of the cold, and from a lack of food. A kind of despairing ruthlessness set in amongst his troops. The pack animals died in steep snow drifts and were eaten by their owners.

According to Gavin Maxwell, writing about this time in his wonderful book *Lords of the Atlas*, hundreds of men died daily and were left unburied in the snow, stripped of the little clothing they had. If their companions did trouble themselves to bury the dead, those not-yet-dead could find themselves on the wrong side of the need to move on.

He tells of an incident in which a man was badly wounded, the camp a long way off, and his companions didn't want the trouble of carrying him there.

So they dug his grave, and began to push him in. He naturally protested. "I am not dead," he cried, "don't you see I am living?" "Be quiet," said a companion, "you were killed at least an hour ago. Don't you realise that you are dead?" The poor man still cried out as the earth covered him and put an end to his protestation and his life.

As the progress struggled on, and their number became fewer and fewer, one thing that was given priority was the heavy Krupp cannon and its equipment which the Sultan regarded as a symbol of his status. By now the Sultan himself was seriously ill and would die before reaching Marrakech on the other side of the mountains.

Madani knew from his spies of the approach of the Sultan and saw his opportunity. He summoned all his people to contribute food and delights and he himself set out to rescue the failing Sultan and what remained of his army.

They were brought to Telouet and treated to days of feasting and celebration.

Maxwell describes the scene.

An endless banquet at which course succeeds course – spice chickens and pigeons, couscous, a whole row of sheep and kebabs and Armen pastries and sweet mint tea long after the guests can eat no more, lasted all through the night; swaying, the lines of women dance to the music of their own wild chance; the traditional boy dancers, with painted faces and white robes drawn tight at the waist by gold embroidered belts, dance to the tambourines and the clicking of copper castanets on their fingers; in the courtyard a huge fire of juniper logs lit the battlements of the castle.

It must have appeared to the Sultan and his followers as if they had found paradise. In his gratitude he made Madani his personal Khalifa, in nominal control of all the tribes between the High Atlas and the Sahara. Probably more usefully and more practically he gave him modern weapons and his Krupp cannon, instantly bestowing enormous military and psychological power upon the inscrutable chief.

The journey to Telouet was the first example on that trip of 'Berber or Moroccan Time'.

Time in the Atlas Mountains is not a rigid government-controlled concept or even for that matter particularly an astronomical one. Nor is itinerary. Questions like: How far? How long? When? are answered as much by reference to the questioner's state of mind and motivation than information on a watch or a map. Which is fair enough.

The journey from Imlil to Telouet turned out to be about seven hours. We drove along through seemingly endless twisting roads before joining what Moha informed me was a military road established with French assistance. Its recent construction, however, made little difference to the speed of our progress as huge, slow moving roadbuilding trucks humphed, growled and rumbled up steep inclines and precipitous corners. Later, I would find that the whole of the Atlas Mountains through the Anti-Atlas to the desert was marked by an endless roadbuilding project, something more than one cynical Berber implied was being done to take the wealth more easily out of the region.

For most of the journey, I sat in the back of the 4x4 whilst Moha gave navigational instructions to the amiable Ahmed, the driver from the Kasbah who had picked me up from the airport the previous day. I sat and dozed, trying not look over the vertiginous edges as Moha egged Ahmed on to overtake old trucks and mule carts piled high with gas bottles and watermelons.

We stopped after a few hours at a little mountain village on the way up the Tichka Pass to get supplies. Almost at the crest of the pass, it seemed a resting point on the way up for vehicles, mostly old French saloons and trucks, to stop and get their breath back. Its main street bustled with snorting Peugeots, mules, coughing Citroëns, donkeys and rheumy Renaults. Along it ran two rows of open-fronted shops, some of them with white chipped tiled stands in front. Upon these stood long metal open barbecues cooking tagine and kebabs. The tagines waited in terracotta pots with an incongruous orange on their lids.

The carcasses of goats and sheep hung outside the dark interiors of shops selling an eccentric mix of sandals, sweet biscuits and sacks of couscous. Smoke lingered in the air and the exhaust fumes of all the trucks and cars mingled with it. A man in an old yellow tabard, ancient trousers and plimsolls directed cars into spaces and out again. He seemed to be a self-appointed traffic attendant who received the occasional tip for his troubles. Moha went off to buy stuff and I got out and stood and breathed in the smells of cooking, exhaust and charcoal, revelling in the noise and the chaos and the colour and the dirt.

No doubt about it – I was back on the road again.

Over lunch, I chatted for a while to Moha, feeling it was very important to get to know him. After all he was going to be my one and only conversational companion for more than three weeks! For Berber people, he was quite tall, although shorter than me, with typical black curly hair and a wide grin. To look at he was a typical modern local guide, slim, wearing 'western' T-shirts, fashionable shades and walking trousers but sticking with the open sandals worn in this region whatever the terrain.

Usually around his neck was draped a Berber/Tuareg desert *shesh*, a long hand-dyed indigo blue scarf which can also double as a turban and face cover when the heat gets cruel and the wind burns. He smoked regular, unfiltered Gauloises cigarettes, and the rich, dark almost burned-rubber smell of its Syrian tobacco would bring a hesitant tag-along aroma of the old French Metro to the whole of our trip.

A university graduate, he spoke French, German, Arabic, pretty good English and of course his native Berber[4].

The relationship between travelling companions is an odd one, similar perhaps to actors cast in a play, relative strangers sharing an intimate narrative. I was the reason Moha was undertaking this long journey and he was the means for us to get there and perhaps for me to survive. Given that he was younger, fitter, more experienced than me, that he understood the terrain, the language and indeed the risks through which we were passing, then my weaknesses would be a concern for him.

We would, over the course of the journey, become close but at this point we were both perhaps seeking the common ground through which we could build trust and understanding.

We chatted about families but these were not topics that proved deeply fruitful. It was only when I started to talk

---

[4] Throughout this book I have used the commonly understood term Berber for the people and their language. More correctly a Berber is Amazigh, the Berbers are Imazighen and the language is mostly Tamazight.

about why I was here and in particular my affection for Berber people and their culture that we started to connect.

I told him that I was fascinated to discover that Amazigh, the Berber word for 'Berber' meant freedom.

"Freeman," he corrected me, before explaining that they were people who were proud of their independence, their history and their culture, something which until very recently had been restricted and eroded by both the Arab-dominated Moroccan elite and previously by the French.

In hesitant English (this was not the vocabulary that a guide would usually need with his followers) he told me that on the south-east side of the Atlas Mountains the Berbers had always lived easily amongst and with others. In the old settlements along the Draa Valley there was usually a Jewish quarter with a synagogue and, outside of the walls, the Jewish cemetery would lie alongside the Moslem one. It was a meeting point for all travellers and peoples and Berbers had understood this.

Setting off again, we abandoned the French military road and turned off towards Telouet. Until this point the road had been okay, albeit of differing widths and with tightly bent hairpins which had left at least one truck on its side. But here the road started to crumble and get a little more vague before turning into a long single track that made only a half-hearted attempt to be a road at all and in several places gave up completely.

As we bounced and juddered, sometimes slowing to walking pace I noted not for the first time the extraordinary colouring of the weathered dirt and soil that surrounded me. I passed the time trying in my mind to find the perfect word or phrase for the colours that I saw - a mental game I would use for the rest of the trip to take my mind off sore feet or knees or thirst. Here I saw verdigris, the copper rust rock containing minerals ground down by heat, frost and furious spring flooding.

Telouet, when we arrived, surprised me. Most of the Berber villages I had seen up in the High Atlas consisted of relatively narrow streets very much shaped by the contours of the land. Telouet's flat and wide main street was flanked on either side by low one- and two-storey dusky apricot buildings from which occasionally hung a sign advertising Maroc Telecom, or Coke. Some were shuttered by the metal doors usually painted in a pastel colour you see all over Morocco but some opened up to little dark interiors selling cigarettes, or cooking oil. There was a café, outside of which bright red and green plastic chairs melted in the sun. It reminded me of nothing so much as a Mexican dirt town in an old spaghetti western. I half expected to see a large ball of tumbleweed roll slowly down the track. I am sure that the Glaoui brothers would have appreciated Calvera the bandit leader in The Magnificent Seven who believed that the poor were only there to be exploited.

The kasbah of the Glaoui was at the edge of Telouet. It was the geographical fulcrum of the Lords of the Atlas, the centre from which this minor hill tribe came, with ruthless flamboyance, to dominate the southern half of Morocco if not whole of the country in a few short years. I saw it now in the middle distance, dark and lonely.

My assumption had been that we would meet with the mules that would accompany our trip somewhere on the outskirts of the village the next morning and that we would walk back to the kasbah in the morning. I was wrong.

I was in Morocco, and the arcane ways in which it moves still remained true. Instead, and surprisingly, we left Telouet, turning away from the kasbah.

"Are we stopping at the Kasbah, Moha?" I asked.

"Yes, that is a good idea," said Moha enigmatically as we drove on, taking an increasingly decrepit track between an angled rocky outcrop and a steepish drop, a kind of rolled, holed switchback route.

I asked Moha where we were going.

"Just a little further – maybe a few minutes."

Moroccan time.

We drove on. I have no Berber language but I could sense in the chatter in the front two seats the rising anxiety of Ahmed the driver as Moha spurred him on through seemingly impossible driving obstacles, at one time squeezing between a cliff face and a huge fallen boulder with a centimetre to spare on each side of the car.

'A few minutes' became many more and three or four villages were edged through. Then suddenly we stopped, up a dirt and rock track to small village of narrow streets and shuttered houses outside a small Moroccan ... auberge I guess. Someone came out from inside and began to unload everything and we all got out.

Thirty minutes later I found myself lying on the bed in my room gazing through the open French doors across a tiled terrace to a lush green flat valley and the sharp fractured slopes of the mountains. A lizard was sunning itself on the beam supporting the terrace roof. Ahmed had departed to make his way gingerly back.

I had no idea where I was.

It was ever thus in Morocco – the only viable strategy is surrender. The only thing I was certain of was that I was not going to Telouet this day or probably the next.

Chapter 3: Cake or Death?

So no Telouet today.

I had chatted to Moha the night before and we decided that a trip back to the Kasbah would just take away a day and that it was time to hit the road. The confusion made me smile. Whenever you read about expeditions such as this, so often you find the author is overtly 'in charge', making decisions with absolute clarity, while his – and it is always 'his' – followers and supporters strive to fulfil them.

I have never found this to be so. Ultimately any progress is achieved through a fog of poor translation, cultural ignorance, misunderstanding and conflicting demands. Moha had asked - again – what I wanted from the trek. My answer: get to the sand-dunes near the Algerian border; if possible, find a tribe of dwarfs; look for the ghosts of old warlords who were sticking heads on the walls of their fortresses in 1947; and, underpinning all this, keep both of us alive.

Over to you, Moha!

The thought made me consider my relationship to Moha. Not surprisingly the world over is full of what I call the 'slow -no' or the 'negative-affirmative', by which local people say 'yes', as in 'yes' I understand, 'yes' I agree, 'yes' I will do, to a foreigner who has just made a request that (a) doesn't take into account important local knowledge, (b) doesn't really make sense and, (c) is impossible anyway. They do this not out of laziness or ignorance but largely out of a disposition to be agreeable and most likely an unwillingness to point out the breath-taking stupidity of what they have just been asked to do.

Alongside Berber time, slow-no was the source of confusion, stress and let me face it, great fun through all the days that followed. My travels have taught me to be okay with this. The point of a good adventure is the unreliability of its plans at any time. So, I had to rely on Moha to get the gist of what I was looking for and let happenstance happen. This has worked well in the past; rigid goals ignore the unfolding of the universe.

At about 7:30am the mules arrived along with their owners Muhammad and Hassan, who was also going to be the cook for the trek. We shook hands and smiled at each other. Muhammad was the older, stocky, with an amiable face, a neat moustache and short, grey hair. Hassan was younger with an age difficult to guess although I found out later that he had children. Wiry, with a more pointed face, he wore a baseball cap. Neither spoke any English but a little French of which I had even less.

Muhammad had an imperturbable air about him and throughout the adventure rarely seemed particularly fazed about anything. Hassan less so. What I had not really taken on board was the reality of this expedition to others and the impact that it might have upon them. Shamefully self-absorbed in my own challenge, I only gradually came to understand how ambitious this journey was for them too and just how far from home and outside their comfort zone they would be.

Unexpectedly with them was a beautiful although slightly fly (not flea) ridden golden retriever and a small child.

The mules waited patiently while we loaded up their wicker panniers with tents, bags, and boxes of food and of course plenty of water. The load on each seemed huge but I have seen in the past mules carry much more. They really are special beasts, thoughtful, immensely strong and patient. The care they constantly received over the days ahead from Hassan and Muhammad, whose livelihood depended upon them, was reassuring,

I asked Moha if the dog and the child were coming with us.

"Only the dog," he said, "the child belongs to the owner of the auberge."

"I thought Moroccans didn't really like, let alone want to keep dogs," I said.

"No, they don't," he replied.

"So, who does is it belong to?" I asked.

"Nobody really," said Moha, "but he seems to have come with Muhammad."

It seems that Berber dogs have inherited the same independent state of mind as Berber people themselves.

And so, leaving the little village of dwellings made of mud and straw blocks we started up the long winding track into the High Atlas Mountains, aiming to get to Lake Tamda, which is at about 2700m, by lunchtime. Then, after taking a break for about an hour, walk for another couple hours and find somewhere to camp for the night. The previous evening

I had chatted to Moha and said that I was good for six hours of walking a day, but perhaps for the first three days, because of the altitude and getting into my stride, we should not push ourselves too hard.

A slow-no? Moha had agreed whilst probably in his mind thinking 'you must be joking, have you seen how far we have to go?' It was probably the shape of things to come therefore when I found myself eleven and a half hours later crashing down onto the ground, having staggered into the camp a few minutes earlier.

The morning started well enough. The path was steep and rocky and we were already setting off at an altitude of 2000m which always gives me a bearable headache for a couple of days. But most of the weight was on the mules, not me, and I kept my stride shorter and slower than normal, the technique I learnt years ago from my old Berber friend Ibrahim who used to joke that 'you Europeans don't really understand physics if you take the same stride length going up a steep slope as you would along the flat ground'. I revelled in being back out in these glorious mountains, always counterpointed between the rough steep bare slopes of the peaks on which a few juniper bushes cling for survival and the rich green fertile narrow valleys which the Berber people tend with almost obsessive and cooperative care. And forming a margin between the two, the shrub and cactus and gnarled pine all coming to life in the gorgeous outpouring of early summer exuberance where even the toxic Oleander joined in the fun. Moha told me that the purple flowers were kept in the bedrooms of the Lords and the Pachas of the region to keep down the insects.

As the morning wore on, we started to cross a long high plain surrounded on all sides by the mountains. Randomly, huge boulders, the size and almost the shape of shipping containers lay around us. It was very hot and we all got strung out over quite a distance. Moha always walked quite a way ahead, sometimes almost out of sight. I felt myself getting frustrated with this and it was a frustration that waxed and waned for the whole of the trip. For a moment I had visions of more than three weeks of a kind of solitude in which I tramped across mountain and desert in pursuit of his receding figure. This and the fact that the four-hour walk to the lake turned out to be more than five and half left me feeling somewhat despondent.

The lake when we got there was austerely beautiful and strange. At 2600 metres above sea level, it is the highest lake in Morocco.

We stopped on its banks. And whilst Hassan and Muhammed unloaded the mules and busied themselves with preparing some food, I slumped to the ground and lay on one of the old mats that were laid across the backs and panniers of the mules when we were on the move.

Staring at bluest of skies, I became aware of my own irritation. I laughed at myself as I lay in the sun exhausted, not daring to move, since even a thought of movement seemed to create a spasm of cramp somewhere in my body. The truth was I was a bit worried about three weeks with Moha if we didn't build some rapport. As the days passed, though, and through the many conversations we had about Berber culture, his family, the Atlas Mountains, the history of Morocco, the story of the dog who joined us and the jokes that were shared in the evenings and at lunch, we became good friends and were able to talk straight to each other about the challenges we faced. I grew to accept that the walking ahead, given the huge distance we had to cover in very tough conditions, was a ruthless but necessary pace setting.

But at this particular stage of the trek and for the next few days I had not achieved the level of detachment and sang-froid necessary to properly appreciate this insight.

The lake itself, shimmering through numerous shades of green, mirrored a rocky landscape. With a convex and concave shore, it was almost kidney shaped, although elongated. In this bare, almost vegetation-free upland, steep rubble-strewn slopes ran down into still waters. I wondered what could possibly breathe or live where plants could not fall and soil could not wash in? One could not imagine how a fish, or any other living thing could exist under its enigmatic placid surface.

As I lay on the ground, hat over my face watching the world from under its brim, the dog walked into the waters and stood in the lake up to its belly enjoying the cool as it brought a little bacteria and muckiness to what lay below. Moha came up to me and gave me a glass of incredibly sweet mint tea which I sipped and let the sugar hit my system like a recreational drug. Muhammad followed and set down a tray between us. On it was an old shiny metal tea pot with a curved spout and an incredibly hot handle, containing more tea. I drank two more glasses quickly and, as long as I didn't move, started to feel better.

"Berber whisky!" said Moha. "It's good to drink when it is hot."

The dog, still in the lake, sat down in it and looked at us happily.

"We should give the dog a name," I said "if he's going to come all the way to the desert with us. I think we should call him Henry."

"That's a good name," replied Moha, "but I think his name is Black!"

"I didn't think Berbers gave their animals names," I grumbled.

"They don't," said Moha, "but they have."

"Why have they called him Black, Blond would make more sense!" Moha laughed but didn't say anything and so I never did find out why he was called Black. Perhaps it was an example of Berber irony.

After about an hour of trying to move as little as possible to avoid provoking the random attacks of cramp in unexpected parts of my body, eating the inevitable Berber salad (a tin of sweetcorn, chopped cucumber, chopped tomatoes, grated beetroot, grated carrot, slices of orange, a slice of cheese and fish from a tin), we set off again.

We walked along the side of the lake then across a broad flat plain strewn with boulders, some absolutely huge and standing distinct to the landscape as if dropped from the sky. Smaller rocks kept man and mule watching their feet. Steep slopes and vertical cliffs rose on both sides of us. Ahead of us in the distance similar high peaks and cliffs stood tall, making the valley seem as if it was a cul-de-sac. I assumed that there was some way round as I plodded on through the heat of the early afternoon. For a while Moha walked alongside me pausing occasionally to look questioningly at slopes to our right.

"Are you looking for the way?" I asked.

Moha pointed out a long, loose scree slope with a steepish section we would have to scramble up to get to the ridge above.

"We can go up here," he said, "but it is a bit technical, or we can go around but that is much, much further."

"Your choice," I said, "but I am happy to give it a go."

Moha changed his mind a couple of times but in the end we scrambled and clambered to the top of the ridge. Up there looking east, I found a fabulous view of the lower slopes of the High Atlas Mountains across a plain disappearing into shimmering haze and on the far, far horizon a thin purple, grey smudge that indicated the start of the Anti-Atlas Mountains. The distance looked enormous and yet I knew that reaching those mountains would only be around a third of my journey.

I was trying to capture the sense of distance through my camera when Moha disappeared. I knew he couldn't have gone further on down the other side because it was a vertical drop of some distance and I figured he must have continued along the ridge which continued in the direction of the end of the valley. I set off in what I guessed was the right direction and a few minutes he suddenly reappeared.

"We should go back," he said, "it is too technical."

"How long will it take to go the other way?" I asked

"Oh, about two or three hours." My heart sank. It was day one and I was already feeling weary. I really hated the idea of retracing steps.

"How technical?"

"Very."

"Show me," I said.

We clambered to the edge of the ridge. Some distance below us I could see a rough and ready route around the side of the mountain levelling out somewhat after a while to cross through a zigzag route down towards a flatter expanse of grass and bush. To get to the route, though, there was a series of short, maybe four-metre vertical climbs to a ledge, followed by another and then several more.

I considered my options carefully. I was tired and had some chance of falling off. In England the descent would have involved ropes and helmets and things. And apart from those sessions on a climbing wall with Richard, I am not a climber. On the other hand, walking back along the ridge and the scrambling down a long scree slope and then a two- to three-hour walk to a point I could see below me seemed the worse choice. Not for the first time in my life I weighed up the distance between potential extinction and feeling more knackered and found it much narrower than might be expected. (I once decided it would be better to die in the snow on the Mer de Glace on the slopes of Mont Blanc than struggle any more in waist deep soft snow to the exit via a bubble lift some distance away.)

Remembering the rather wonderful Eddie Izzard sketch in which a rather wet and flaccid Church of England Inquisition offered its victims 'cake or death', I muttered:

"Cake or Death it is."

Not surprisingly Moha looked non-plussed.

"Let's go down!" I said.

With Berber nimbleness, Moha climbed down first to each ledge, often facing outwards into the void and I somewhat more cautiously followed. To tell the truth, apart from one heart-in-my-mouth moment when the rock I was clinging to came away and bounced past Moha's head, I rather enjoyed it.

When we got to the sloping path. Moha looked at me with a note of approval.

"Ha!" I thought, "I may be a fat bloke with a dodgy knee, but don't underestimate me!"

And we set off again, with normal service soon being resumed as Moha strode off into the distance. I briefly caught up with him as we met back up again with Muhammad and

Hassan, who had ridden the long way around on the mules with Black trotting alongside them. It was now about six o'clock and we had, apart from the stop by the lake at lunchtime, been walking since before nine that morning and it had been very hot, much hotter than I expected, most of the day. Around us was a grassy patch of level ground overlooking a valley and the receding line of mountains and valleys coloured olive, auburn and smoky blue and gilded by the lowering sun.

"This looks a great place to make camp," I suggested.

"We just need to go a little further down into the valley there," said Moha.

"Are you sure?" I pathetically asked but Moha had stridden on.

And so we set off again with the others. The route down was steep, twisting and strewn with boulders of all sizes, making it impossible to establish any sort of rhythm to my stride. This is precisely the terrain that aggravates my battered old knee and every second step became very painful with pains shooting up into my groin and even into the small of my back. The temperature still remained stubbornly hot.

I grew frustrated and battled with myself to not dissolve into resentment and anger as I struggled to keep up. It took over two more hours to get down to a small flat piece of ground next to a waterfall. Here, at last, we camped. I was more exhausted than I have ever felt in my life. On the way down I think I had become so tired and dehydrated that I slipped on several occasions, sending myself sprawling. I think also I was slightly hallucinating. I saw that the rocks lying on the ground were coloured by various minerals, some shining red like garnets, white diamonds glowing in incredible colours in the evening light. I bent and picked up a small rock about the size of my thumb. It was the most exquisite gold green copper colour and seemed to glow as if lit from within. In the morning when I looked at it again it was a nondescript grey. The magic had disappeared, and I threw it away.

I took off my boots and cleaned my feet and then lay back watching the evening moon slowly crest the ridge above us. Hassan busied himself cooking dinner as Muhammad tended to the mules. Moha sat on a rock a little way away smoking a cigarette whilst Black was curled up asleep, weary too.

No question about it: I was worried. That day we had hiked over twenty miles, walked up and crested two ridges from the valley below at around 3000 metres and trekked for over eleven hours and even at 8.30pm the heat lingered on. The idea that I was facing three weeks of this seemed impossible. I had tried to talk to Moha about it and he had said that it would be easier the next few days but I suspected that he was just saying that to make me feel better.

In the end I came to the practical conclusion that I was just going to have to suck it up. There was no way I could retreat from here and feeling sorry for myself was not going make anything any easier.

So I crawled into my little tent, leaving my head sticking out to catch the cool of the breeze. And anyway, I thought, this is without doubt the start of the adventure. What the next days would bring was impossible to know and, somewhat comforted by this thought, I fell asleep.

Chapter 4: The Strangeness of the Strange

I awoke at sunrise – as I did for most of the trek – and basked in the knowledge that a sign of early rapport between Moha and me was that neither of us relished a rushed and brutal start. I lay there reviewing my physical state after the exertions of the previous day and found myself much less battered than anticipated. All in working order, I stuck my head out of my tent and looked around.

The air was that subtle fragrant cool that lingers after night and before the sun bears down. The mules shifted in the fresh air as if committing it to memory for the day ahead. Muhammad and Hassan simultaneously appeared from the large square tent with the heavy struts like scaffolding poles in which they had slept, and we ate. Muhammad headed off to feed the mules and Hassan to make breakfast. There was a pop and a hiss as the old stove was lit.

And so we set off on day two, me feeling quite prepared and determined. It turned out to be another long 20 miler, though much easier than the day before. The descents were more benign and, seeing Moha set off a couple of hundred metres in front of me, I plugged in my iPod and settled down to cover the miles. From the camp we walked along a wide, desolate plateau picking our way over dried stream beds, rock and mud where salt crystals, like forgotten snow, glistened in the hot sun. I gingerly tasted the water. Sure enough it was salty. The crystals had been washed down from the salt mountains behind us where the old salt mines quietly hid their stories.

The notion of salt mines tolls a sombre note wherever they are found. From Rome to Siberia they were places of punishment and degradation. Subterranean tunnels of despair, hidden from sight and relief. It has always been a dividing line amongst people. To be 'below the salt' in the halls of the powerful was to be denied the seasoning and marked as of little worth and value.

I became more aware that the mountains through which I walked were olive green not from vegetation, but from the colouring of the earth itself and, within this, patches and sections of tan, sand, sienna and wheat colours betrayed a complex and ancient mineral cocktail. Away from the dried-up riverbed the path was made of baked mud, rich in, I guess, iron and coloured somewhere between coral, peach and brick punctuated with only the vegetation growing, half footballs of a spiky grey-green wire-grass. Blocks of mud, fired by a thousand suns were criss-crossed by snaky lines and grooves like the skin on the palm of an old hand, telling a story and perhaps foretelling a future. And around me the summits rose like old stone warriors, weird and steep, with near vertical faces folded as if giant hands had taken enormous layers of plasticine and gathered and pleated them.

As I trudged along, it felt more and more as if I was walking into the landscape rather than just across it. It was as if the simple two-dimensions of 'amongst mountains' was crumbling, gaining more dimensions and a more intense, weird way of seeing where I was emerged. When I was a kid, magazines used to market 'X-Ray Specs', the purchaser of which would be able to see the bones of their hands or beneath the clothes of the voluptuous lady in the advert. I felt as if I was being so endowed, albeit in a deeper, more creative and almost spiritual way.

This is a naked landscape, I thought. The very DNA of the place is on view. A German traveller during the 19th Century in the region found a 'pass five paces wide, with perpendicular marble walls ... which glistened in some places as smooth as if artistically polished and reflected rays of every possible colour' in which he found a carbonic acid spring through which 'large bubbles continually rise to the surface, and in drinking the water it effervesces in one's mouth like champagne.'

I kept glancing backwards to the awesome grandeur of the mountains from which we had descended, trying to work out where we had crested the range and begun our descent. Moha, who had slowed down beside me pointed out the ridge and face we had made our way down. It seemed now insignificant against the towering massifs behind it.

We walked for a while along the course of a river which was broad and wide and, except for little rivulets, bone dry. The riverbed was sculpted into little dusky red peaks and troughs, presumably by the swirling spring waters. In a raised part of the river a group of ground squirrels were watching us warily, their striped tails hovering in anticipation of threat.

"Berber people like to eat them," said Moha. "They're quite good."

I entered into a long and convoluted explanation about the rivalry between red and grey squirrels and how some people in England were trying to persuade others to eat the grey ones and that I had seen them for sale in Hexham market. And anyway we called them ground squirrels, and there had been a cartoon series about chipmunks on television in Britain years ago.

Moha had the grace to pretend to follow this ramble. I do this occasionally; a kind of culturally-blind loquaciousness overtakes me. I once spent two hours in a tent with three Berber men trying to explain the causes and course of the 100 years' war with France, with my friend 'Brahim acting as an interpreter. It was clear five minutes in and even I was dimly aware that the other two were hurling daggers at the idiot who had asked me what the English thought of the French. But I guess having started I feel compelled to continue whatever the cost to others.

Perhaps to change the debate from *Sciurus vulgaris* vs *Sciurus carolinensis*, Moha resumed a conversation we had started the day before about the fate of the Berbers in North Africa. He told me that it was only recently that their language had been recognised and taught in schools and that they were still in many ways marginalised from mainstream Moroccan society. He also said that there were musicians and writers who had written and sung and argued for the place of this ancient people in the world and who had been murdered or mysteriously just disappeared.

I told him about Gavin Maxwell and his book *The Lords of the Atlas*, a book which for a while had been banned in Morocco as subversive.

He was really intrigued, saying that Berber history was not taught or celebrated much and most of the things you read about were usually wrong or biased. The only time the Arabs called anything Berber, he told me, was when they wanted to sell it: hence Berber carpets, Berber knives, Berber lamps, which mostly weren't Berber at all.

Our conversation paused and Moha resumed his walking position up front as we started to climb away from the riverbed, almost doubling back on ourselves to cross another ridge. As we wound up the long path out of the valley I mused again on the remoteness of where I was. Over several hours we passed through no more than two little settlements of houses made from mud, straw and wood and didn't see another human being apart from an old goatherd watching over a scattered bunch of little silky-haired goats, a woman in a brightly coloured Kaftan staring impassively from a door and an old man curled up on a mat asleep in the shade. All the time the huge peaks of the High Atlas loomed over us and somewhere amongst them the mysterious Salt Mountains, from which salty streams carried cheap jewellery to lie in the dirt along the way.

We ate lunch in a steep mostly dry gully through which a tiny stream anxiously made its way – almost disappearing in one or two places to get out of the noonday sun. Lunch would follow the same routine more or less all of the whole trip. First find somewhere, anywhere that offered a little shade (although for today and for several more to follow there was none); lift off the large wicker baskets from the mules and let them wander a little way to find water if there was any; untie the old cotton covered foam ground mats from the baskets and lay them as close as possible to any shade on offer. Moha and I, who both always walked, would then sink gratefully down onto them, me untying and taking off my shoes and socks, turning the socks inside out to let them air in the heat. I would always carefully clean my feet with the almost fanatical belief that if I cherished them, I would avoid the blisters that had caused problems on a previous trip during a hot dry summer when the ground was hard as iron. It was something that more or less worked.

I would then lie back and shade my face with my old Tilly hat and fall asleep. I have discovered on previous trips that lunch is something that Berbers don't like to rush. There are never freeze-dried foods, protein bars or sachets of gloop to be consumed. We carried, in old cardboard boxes and raffia sacks and bags, a variety of foodstuffs: dried lentils; couscous; tins of sweet corn; root vegetables such as potatoes; carrots and beetroot; tins of oily fish; tomatoes; cucumber; packets of dried milk; coffee; packets of soft cheese in foil which miraculously never seemed to melt; sugar cubes (essential to a tea drinking Berber); a yellow box of Lipton; a box of Coco Pops; and a jar of jam. There was a large can of cooking oil and bottles of water for drinking and big plastic water carriers for cooking – although the Berber guys drank happily from both they were very insistent I didn't try. And finally, infusing the whole of the supplies with the redolent, exotic and the arcane smell of the Maghreb, bags of Ras el Hanout, a blend of spices with an almost infinite number of ingredients and recipes, imbued with the history and story of each family who makes it, but almost always including coriander, cumin, cardamom, chilli, turmeric, cloves, ginger and paprika. The smallest tickle of it on the breeze always and instantly transports me to mental space of heat, dust, colour and quarter-tone music.

But before any cooking commences or preparation begins, mint tea is made. It is very easy to believe in this day of significant tourism to Morocco that the whole palaver of making mint tea is somehow put on to entertain the visitor. But nothing could be further from the truth. I've been coming to Morocco for twenty years and watched the whole elaborate ritual in the remotest and least visited parts of the country.

Often undertaken in the dirt, the dust and the mud, it has always been with the sort of fanatical attention to ceremony and tradition that would grace the most exquisite Japanese Sado tea ceremony. The water is boiled in a large battered old tin kettle, then poured into a bulbous teapot made of stainless steel or chrome standing on little legs, with a long curving spout and a domed lid. I'm told the tea is similar to gunpowder tea. I have to say, being a bit of a fan of gunpowder tea, it tastes much darker and smokier than that. In fact, later on the trek when we ran out of mint and we had 'mint tea' without it, I complained to Moha that the tea tasted of tobacco! After the tea is allowed to brew a little, mint leaves, sometimes still on a twig, are added to the pot. There then commences the rather mysterious part of the ceremony where the tea is poured into smallish glasses. As it is poured the trick is to raise your arm and thereby hold the teapot just over the glass to maybe half a metre above, letting the liquid fall through the air into the glass. The glassful of tea is then held up to the light and inspected carefully and then poured back into the teapot whereupon the action may be repeated several times. I must have seen this deeply important and reverential practice hundreds of times but I have no idea really what the tea maker is looking for. I have been told there is some process of aeration going on which can be seen by careful inspection. Or indeed some clarity of liquid is being checked but these have tended to be in the accounts of quick glance travel writers rather than people who have undertaken deeply anthropological research into the phenomenon. I asked Moha once. He said it was to see whether enough bubbles were being created so that when the tea glass was drunk in sandy and dusty conditions grains of sand and small insects would be trapped on the surface and easily removed by the swirl of fingernail. To be honest I have no idea whether he was teasing me or not. It remains a bit of a mystery, but then again nor do I know what big-bellied Englishmen who lift their real ale to the hazy light of the bar are looking for either.

So, hot as it was that day, and even with a fierce sun, I knew that there was no such thing out here as a quick lunch, so I drank some warm water and dozed for about twenty minutes. I awoke with that strange sensation of being stared at. The voyeur turned out to be a goat standing on a rock opposite me who was looking at me with its head cocked to one side. The stare was long and unblinking. I stared back. Now goat's eyes are very weird: the pupil is a horizontal slit like a tiny post-box set in amber. Scientists claim that this is to maximise peripheral vision to watch for predators whilst minimising the glare from the sun above. Whatever, the sensation of being stared by a goat is somehow disconcerting, particularly given this one had auburn sideburns and little horns sprouting from his head. In this state of mutual hypnosis, I recalled reading somewhere that some units of the US army in the 1960s tried training themselves to kill things by telepathy and apparently they used to practise on goats. This fellow with the beautiful face and the alien eyes was impervious to my attempts to make him even doze off a little. My mental straining was interrupted when Muhammad brought me a glass of hot mint tea.

"Shukran," (thank you) I said with one of my few words of Arabic and made a mental resolution to at least learn the Berber for 'thank you' (*tanemmirt*).

Breaking the stare I looked around and the goat wandered off to practise psychic warfare on someone or something else. I took a sip from the hot sweet mint tea and, putting the glass back on the ground, I walked over to a little stagnant puddle.

I pushed aside some of the debris on the surface aside and scooped my hat full of the muddy water and put it back on my head. The water ran down my head on all sides and I relished the momentary release from the heat. As it continued to trickle over my eyes and down the back of neck I saw Moha, Hassan and Muhammad grinning at me. I grinned back with a feeling of cheerful complicity.

Setting off again, we continued to walk up and away from the plain and headed towards a long ridge. Our next destination was Ben Haddou, but that was going to be at least another two days' hike.

Evening saw us reach a hamlet high up amongst barren and burned land which seemed deserted except for an old man with the most incredibly lined face. We camped that night near the deserted ruins of an old kasbah, lonely and forgotten. In the evening light it seemed to glow. Its dusty terracotta walls and roofless halls sat on top of a low mound, the mud from which it was clearly drawn. Behind it ran a steep path up to a ridge which ran along the skyline in a monotone of saffron-grey. Nearby was a splash of bright green from prickly bushes and the occasional gorse which clung to the side of the mound like forgotten antique cushions. Behind the ridge the sky was a pale evening blue. All in all, it was a landscape austere and wonderful, painted with the simplest of palettes.

Apart from tea a few hours earlier with the old woman and child, and the old man who had completely disappeared, we had not seen another human being all day. Yet the crumbling kasbah was a testament to the fact that people had once lived here, and the place held a hundred forgotten stories. And old magic.

We pitched camp in a low-walled enclosure with a post sticking out of the ground in the middle. At harvest time one or more mules would be tethered here and set to work circling the post, threshing the barley and the corn. Our mules, possibly mindful of this, once unloaded soon took themselves to the other side of the wall and watched proceedings over it until Muhammad attached some nosebags of grain and they ambled a little way off to eat in peace.

It grew dark very quickly and Moha, Muhammad and I sat, or rather lay, in the middle of a square tent upon the old rugs and cushions that made up the floor.

The three Berbers each had an old roll mat, one on each closed side of the tent. Here they slept. I had my own tent, a small thing erected just outside. I had toyed with the idea of giving up on that and sleeping in here, but I recognised my monoglot presence would make every conversation slow and difficult.

Moha and I sat chatting and watching Hassan prepare some lentil soup followed by a vegetable tagine all over a rickety one-burner gas stove screwed onto a bent and battered Calor gas bottle. The tent was lit by a couple of head torches and a battery-powered lamp which I had happened to bring. Black lay outside watching us, making no attempt to come in.

In awkward Franglais I asked Hassan if he had children. Two twin boys. We were having a joke - worked tri-lingually and slowly - about who looked the oldest, Muhammad or me, when a young Berber boy suddenly popped his head around the tent door. He looked at us confidently and we stopped talking instantly. Moha asked him what he wanted (presumably). He thrust out a paper bag clenched in his hand. It contained four eggs which he wanted to sell. Where he had come from I couldn't imagine, since there had been no sign of inhabited buildings when we arrived and no light glimmered, howsoever faintly in the enveloping darkness outside.

He was instantly invited in and he sat down between Hassan and Moha and looked around confidently. Hassan poured him a glass of tea and gave him a biscuit. Not for the first time I noticed the way in which giving and receiving is such a natural activity amongst Berbers. Throughout the trip, food, drink, cigarettes, were offered simply and easily and accepted with a nod of the head, perhaps with a smile but never with any theatrical 'oh-I-couldn't-possibly' mock refusal. Hassan chatted to him benignly as he continued to prepare the evening meal, Moha listening in.

"It seems a hard life up here," I said.

"Very hard," replied Moha. "Many young people go to live in the cities like Marrakech."

"Do you live there?" I asked.

"Only during the week," said Moha.

The boy was fed well, supplied with several pieces of soft cheese in foil, paid handsomely for the eggs and disappeared off into the night. I noticed that Muhammad saw him safely away in the darkness.

Later that night I thought about the boy and the way he had just appeared out of nowhere. I thought about the Salt Mountains and the mineral rich landscape. Thought about the remote, threatening mountain passes in which fierce, wild peoples would have demanded tribute from exhausted travellers, or simply killed and robbed them if that had seemed more expedient. And the desolation. Somewhere out in the darkness I heard the strange unrecognisable cry of a wild animal. Black growled a warning and across the valley a dozen or so unexpected dogs barked out a reply. Emptiness in a place like this is not an absolute; it is a quality of the unknown. In a place such as this, in the strangeness of the strange, it would be perfectly possible to hide a tribe of dwarfs or for an imagination to put them there.

Chapter 5: Freedom's Another Word

The next day we set off in the accelerating heat on a long trek upwards. For a while we walked together higher and higher, Muhammad and Hassan walking alongside the patient swaying and swishing mules, Moha as usual a little way ahead and me following behind, my walking poles clicking and thumping on the ground. Black trotted amiably alongside. He seemed now an almost inevitable part of our troupe.

Despite the Moroccan indifference to dogs, Hassan had fed Black some scraps at breakfast and Muhammad had made sure he had water. There was something rather noble about Black. He did not beg or bother. He did not 'intrude' but rather, sure of his worth, accepted gifts as ones offered between equals.

We stopped near a solitary dwelling in the middle of nowhere for a while to drink some water, eat some dates and take a breather. It seemed to be inhabited and I wondered, not for the first time, how in this desolate wilderness, someone could survive. There is no soil, precious little water, extreme heat, no chance to grow a crop. And perhaps as pertinently, no apparent reason to.

From out of the gloomy interior of the lodging appeared a stout Berber woman carrying a toddler in a sling on her back. She shouted a greeting to us, and Moha replied. A few minutes later the woman reappeared with a silver tray, a teapot of mint tea, and some glasses. Placing them on ground amongst us she started an animated conversation with Moha and Hassan whilst Muhammad fed the mules.

I have noticed many times that Berber women, though Muslim, do not tend to display as much reticence in talking to strangers as I often find with poorer Arab women. She was, however, very firm in declining my request to take her photograph and, although she was happy enough for me to take her daughter's picture, her daughter herself was equally firm in declining the suggestion, making this clear by putting her head on the ground and screaming whenever I pointed my camera in her direction.

Moha gave the lady a few coins and we set off again marching through the desolation and the heat until several hours later, stumbling and staggering along an interminable switchback path covered in rocks of all sizes, we arrived exhausted at a Berber gîte.

When Moha had mentioned this as a possible destination that evening, I had had mixed feelings. Somewhere in the vagueness of my understanding, I had assumed that we would be camping all the way and on hearing that that night we would be staying in accommodation, I felt a bit like we were cheating in some way. I eased my concerns by convincing myself that any decent traveller would never deliberately turn down the opportunity to mix and spend time with local people. And anyway, the accommodation was unlikely to be an over luxurious experience. Which turned out to be true.

We arrived at about dusk. The gîte lay next to a road where a couple of old dusty vans were parked. They both looked like they had been there some time, and no traffic came or went the entire time we were there.

Further up the road a group of men stood round an old truck, relieved of their work by the setting sun. We made our way up a few steps onto a walled terrace surrounded on three sides by a low, two-storey dusky red orange mud brick building. In the middle of the terrace was an orange tree under which Black immediately flopped down and went to sleep. The patron arrived, a youngish man who showed me upstairs to a stone-floored room lit by a single light bulb hanging from the middle of ceiling. On the floor a thin old mattress was placed with a couple of blankets.

"Voici votre lit," he smiled and left me to my *chambre*.

I dumped my bags and walked down to the terrace and wearily half leant on one of the mule bags on the stone seat that ran down one wall. I was desperately thirsty and ate two oranges, sadly noticing the ecstatic impact they had had on me over the last few days starting to diminish. Still thirsty, I collected the dried milk, Nesquik and not quite lukewarm water from one of the saddlebags and made myself a milkshake. I smiled at the incongruity of it – Nesquik chocolate milk is not on my list of regular beverages or those of 'survival community', but in the liquid and carbohydrate deprived state I was probably in, it tasted wonderful. But better was to come. Moha sidled up to me grin on his face.

"I know a man with a beer, do you want one?"

"Yes please!"

"You have a shower, and I will get them to fetch one."

I did not expect a shower either, let alone a beer, but with typical Berber bodging ingenuity the hostelry had found an old hot water tank which they had propped up on some bricks on the flat concrete roof and had lit a wood fire underneath. A pipe led out from tank down through a hole which had been chipped into the concrete roof and then on into a small, tiled room where it emerged from a rusty old showerhead attached to the wall. And it worked!

Anyone who has trekked in the heat and dust for any length of time will relate to the sheer delight standing in a shower getting clean. Returning to the courtyard, the heat dying down to a gentle sultriness, I found a tin of cold Dutch beer waiting for me. My attempts to find out later how and where it had come from were met by typical charming Berber evasiveness.

Muhammad, Hassan and Moha sat in one of the open rooms off the terrace chatting and laughing and slowly making dinner while I sipped beer and thought about the day. It was not a bad start; we had covered more than 60 miles in three days which given the terrain, the heat and the altitude did seem good going. And we were now a long way from ... it is conventional here to say 'civilisation'. That is massively disrespectful to the rich and complex world that exists in and around the Berber mind. The 'familiar' is probably better. And the trouble with the 'familiar' is that we see it even when it isn't there.

On the wall of the hostel entrance as I came in was an unfamiliar sign. It was an inverted U-shape with the shape of another U directly above it and the vertical line dissecting the two. I had asked Moha what it was, as it had appeared on several of the buildings in this small village. It was the Berber letter Z, he had told me, but it also meant 'free men' and represented the 'spirit of Berber people'. As the days went by I noticed the symbol everywhere, on walls, the sides of the buildings and on flags. Usually the flag had three horizontal bands of yellow, green and blue. The blue represents the sea to the north and west, the green the magnificent mountains of the Atlas and the Riff, and the yellow the Sahara desert. The symbol connects the three colours across the middle and is often in a dark red. Compellingly this is not the flag of a nation, or indeed an aspiration to be one. It is about what connects a group of people, a desire to be free and to live in harmony with the land.

As the trek went on, I became more and more aware of the way this idea of freedom shaped so much the way Berber people saw the world. I think this suspicion of remote authority is why I felt so connected to what Berbers stand for us all. It is too easy in the West to assume a naturally ordained progression from tribal chiefs to nations led by kings and emperors, or the gathering strength of the middle classes towards some form of democracy. But this is not ordained. As Maxwell points out 'there appears to exist in the Berber make up some basic inhibition against the forming of large groups' and that any social structure that got too big would subdivide. It was the Glaoui with French backing who imposed a much more feudal structure on the region.

Next morning, we set off, with the mules taking a more circuitous route on the road whilst Moha and I made our way down to the river Ounila through little fields of wheat, alfalfa, and beans. As we reached the riverside we slipped between copses of bamboo and silver birch. The river when we reached it at this point was full of huge boulders washed down by the spring melt. This meant that the going was tricky as regularly we had to clamber over them. We saw a group of Berber women near a small waterfall. They were wearing brightly coloured caftans. One woman, hands on hips, was standing in a large metal tub stepping up and down to wash the clothes. Another was beating and rinsing out clothes on some rocks, another was hanging clothes and sheets off the bushes to dry them in the sunshine. It was a timeless scene. Once again I recalled that taking photographs often offended so I resisted the temptation.

Although the flow of the river at this time of year was quite light, clearly it would have been a spectacular place earlier in the year. Further along its course we gave up scrambling from bank to bank over rocks and instead waded, when necessary, and the cold water on hot feet was beautiful. Birds were singing, frogs croaking and we stopped and stared into a large pool. And there on a ledge at water level in the shade of a big rock was a large turtle. When it sensed us watching it slipped off the rock and into the water and hung around near the bottom of a small pool weighing up its next move. Now I've always been fond of turtles: they are very much 'I've got my life, you got yours' sort of beasts, ponderous and amiable.

Finding the turtle was both unexpected and entrancing. This is the way of adventure: you are hot and you are bothered and the going is grim and then unexpectedly a moment of instant enchantment appears, doubly magical because of its surprise.

And I say 'turtle' on the basis that it was in water and that I supposedly thought distinguishes it from 'tortoise'. I went to the Internet to confirm this on my return and found in fact that it is only sea swimming turtles that are truly turtles, and freshwater swimming turtles are better referred to as terrapins. Except I found that terrapins are generally quite small and this was the size of half a football. Google also informed me that in fact tortoises can, with some reluctance, swim. So in the end I don't really know what it was. Turtle? Tortoise? Terrapin? It gazed up suspiciously at Moha and me, inscrutable and unknowable. And this is also what adventure is about: accepting the ongoing uncertainty of the moment as in 'what did I really see? I guess I'll never know.' That's what makes adventures special.

But I did find out from Mr Google that sea turtles breathe through their bottoms during the winter.

After a couple more hours of wading and scrambling we paused on the bank and sat under a bush to eat an orange. A pair of falcons soared up above the cliffs opposite.

Later we headed away from the river and took a long slog to Ben Haddou through a very hot and strong dry wind blowing in from the desert. I had become very dehydrated and drinking warm water from my Sigg flask didn't seem to help. Fortunately, as the day unfolded the area became slightly more populated with occasional villages which might have a tiny dark shop and some of them even had a fridge. And in these dark places were always a few plastic bottles of yoghurt or sugary fruit drink. I think I'd drunk about three litres of varieties of this gunk by the end of that day - the dry wind coupled with the fruit sugar made my lips stiff like slightly dried plasticine formed, I imagined, into the folded shape of the posterior orifice of a waterfowl.

That afternoon we reached the astonishing Ksar of Ben Haddou, a fortified village standing on and reaching up a large rocky outcrop on the top of which stood a tower. Ben

Haddou is a World Heritage site and an almost perfectly intact example of the ancient settlements that would have risen to meet the long winding caravans that once snaked across the Sahara to rest before embarking upon the hazardous crossing of the High Atlas Mountains via the Tizi'n'Telouet pass.

On the outskirts of the settlement, we parked our mules and belongings at a campsite where we would stay that night and walked towards this remarkable place.

Ben Haddou is now divided into two – the old Ksar being a short walk away from a roadside development of dwellings, cafés, small hotels where the coaches who have driven round of the Atlas Mountains from the coast gather to disgorge their Japanese, French, German, and American tourists to gaze upon a place moved by a time machine from an ancient, twelfth century past.

But they, and you, have already seen it before. If you have watched *Gladiator*, *Kingdom of Heaven*, *Prince of Persia*, *The Mummy* or even that old Hollywood concoction *Sodom and Gomorrah*, then you have seen Ben Haddou. Like a reliable old thespian called out of retirement to ace it with a minor character part that leaves everyone talking, Ben Haddou is a star in many films.

Moha told me that whilst most people live nowadays in the new town, working in the restaurants, cafés and shops that feed tourists, three or four families still live in this mud brick citadel. The walls, buildings and towers that you can see are only about three hundred years old but embody a much more ancient tradition of architecture. Mud brick buildings do not last and all along the trek we would pass through little villages in a constant state of renewal.

The crowds were making their way to their air-conditioned coaches as we walked up to the Ksar and in through one of the great doors as the afternoon edged to twilight. Moha was keen to explain that the jumbled warren of streets and alleyways inside was in fact deliberate, designed to create pinch points and dead ends for any attackers. The second door of the Ksar provided an escape route should this Plan A go wrong.

Walking the battlements, Moha showed me where the caravanserai, a kind of parking ground for the camel trains that wound out of the desert would have been. It was easy to imagine hundreds of camels and their owners resting there, their fires sending sparks into the night sky and their tents glowing from the lights within, the walls of the same showing strange and distorted shadows.

Also, below the walls, Moha pointed out two graveyards, one Muslim and the other Jewish, sitting side by side like old friends. The ancient relationship between Jews and Moroccans on this side of the Atlas Mountains seems to be a complex one and rarely marked with the bitter enmity that can exist elsewhere. (In the whole of Morocco, Jews have been both appointed to high positions in society and government and also ruthlessly persecuted at other times.)

There is a controversial theory that in fact Moroccan Jews were originally Berber/Imazighen converts. Whether this is true or not is doubtful but there is definite evidence of Jewish communities in the region by the 3rd Century and suggestions that they might have been there since 361BCE.

Moha himself was keen to emphasise the cordiality of relationships between Jewish and Berber peoples, witnessed by the fact that many of the former spoke Berber[5].

Looking out as the sun burned into the horizon and the tourists set sail in their buses for their next destination, I could easily imagine that Ben Haddou would have once been like a port; after all, camels are often referred to as 'ships of the desert'. And like all ports it would have been a meeting point for many races. In this place of walls and shadows, in a jumble of clay brick dwellings of all sizes, once lived a vibrant interconnected community of artisans and adventurers where a tapestry of language, religion and ancestry was woven, drawing people in from the vastness and unknowableness of the interior of Northern Africa.

[5] (Tamazight)

Chapter 6: Arrested!

Moha had offered two choices at breakfast. Our next destination was the town of Ouarzazate, the capital of this region, sometimes known as the 'Door to the Desert'. We could get there, he said, either in one exceptionally long day like our previous days so far, or in two less strenuous days.

We decided to hit the road and see how we were doing after a couple of hours, but the idea to me of beasting ourselves today and having a day off in Ouarzazate was enticing. The Kasbah Taourirt at the heart of the city had been owned by Thami El Glaoui and it was rumoured that the famous Krupp cannon from which the Lords of the Atlas built their psychological and military threat would be there.

Getting there in one day offered the opportunity for a rest day and I was not the only one feeling the pace in terms of heat and distance. Hassan, the cook, had grumbled he was *très fatigué* and Black, if we stopped for a moment, immediately found shade and went to sleep.

Leaving Ben Haddou, the landscape was rocky desert now. Ouarzazate sits approximately in the middle of a high plain. Behind us as we walked was the purple horizon of the High Atlas Mountains and in front of us on the opposite horizon, the smaller line of the Anti-Atlas, grey and gold. We followed, most of the day, broad tracks that ran alongside more or less a new tarmacadam road except for crossing a small range of hills.

Within a couple of hours of setting off, Moha and I were sitting in a rickety cafe on the roadside of a small settlement, drinking coffee and reviewing progress. We decided that with the pace we were going and the tedium of the route, we might as well go all the way to Ouarzazate. There the plan was to camp by the river that night and move on to another camp outside the town the following day. This would give us a few hours in the town and also be in a position to make a good start for what would be a tough three or four days crossing the Anti-Atlas.

For a while the way was tedious. Mostly we walked alongside the main road through the grit and dust at its edges. Sweat poured from the band of my Tilly hat and stung the edges of my eyes. The muddy earth, kicked up from the ground beneath my feet, stuck to my face and lips. Heat rose as much from track below as from the burning sun above. Soon the water in my flask was tepid and warm.

As usual Moha kept the pace some distance in front of me and I was left to face my trials on my own.

The landscape was wide, mostly featureless stony desert and scrub.   Except for the occasional diesel-smoking truck, nothing moved but us.

How do you keep going when you're feeling boiled and baked? The landscape monotonous and without promise? My lessons are long and hard learned. You must let go of distance and not fight the frustration of feeling you are not going anywhere fast enough. You have to observe dispassionately the physical discomfort. It's a kind of stoic mindfulness; the only practical thought is to make the next footstep in front of you happen. I sometimes chant to myself "One more less" meaning metre, step or minute to go.

A particular favourite aid of mine is to use lightweight walking poles. By this time on the trek, they had almost permanently become an intimate part of me when walking. Attached to my hands I could use them without thinking and when I didn't need them I instinctively transferred one to the other hand so that they were both carried together, transferring it back equally unconsciously, like dropping a gear, when the occasion demands it.

The great actor Anthony Sher once played Richard the Third, spiderlike, with two crutches permanently attached to his arms. I imagine I looked much the same. People I have walked with sometimes complained about possible injury from my extended reach with pointy things. I'm afraid my response is always to invite them to stand a little further away.

I have tried to find out what the physical advantage of using the poles was by looking up some scientific research on the subject. Irritatingly, all I could find was some pointless data about the use of poles using more muscle groups and offering a whole-body workout. If you're walking 25 miles with temperatures in the mid-30s, a whole body workout is not the reason you use walking poles. The true secret must be in the mechanical advantage of effort to speed or distance.

But perhaps my primary tactic when travelling through the strenuous and mundane is to think about things. Liberated from dealing with the tribulations of life by the simple monotony of my current situation, my brain can happily spend hours ruminating on the philosophical, fanciful and arcane. Our rest stops would then require me to scribble down these thoughts in my ever ready Moleskine notebook.

Perhaps it was just as well then that the brothers Glaoui had given me something to think about as I trudged along that day. Having missed visiting the Kasbah at Telouet I was anxious to make more of an acquaintance with the brothers Glaoui. They glimmer through history like the gangster brothers of London, the Kray twins, in their mixture of cunning, charisma, and cruelty.

At the end of the 19th century and the start of the 20th century, the brothers were leaders of the third most influential tribe in the High Atlas Mountains. With their wealth from the salt mines and their new cannon they were on the up, but hardly pushing for the premier league of despotic villainy. Within a few decades, however, by wanton opportunism, a skill at ingratiating themselves with the ineffectual rulers of Morocco, sometimes unhinged nastiness and perhaps just being in the right place at the right time, they had come to dominate the region and in the end for the younger brother, T'hami, Morocco itself.

Morocco at the time was a place of shifting and turbulent politics with frequent insurrections and gambles for power. In 1902, Madani, Thami's elder brother, had thrown his support behind the imperial army of Sultan Moulay Abdulaziz, as the Sultan struggled to remove the pretender Bou Hamara. The complete failure of this action resulted in Madani being made the scapegoat for a while and ruined.

However, the brothers made their way back to the heights of influence, Madani successfully working to get the then ruler, Moulay Abdulaziz deposed and the new Sultan Moulay Hafid, in his gratitude, making Madani Grand Vizier and Thami Pasha of Marrakesh.

The brothers were engaged in the long-standing Moroccan practice of 'winner takes all' and could expect, if they lost, for all their possessions to be confiscated, their property destroyed, their servants and followers maimed or massacred, their wives and womenfolk abused and sold as slaves and themselves to be killed in one of the various colourful ways practised at that time, including being sawn in half lengthways.

After Madani's death in 1918, the French, following the colonial practice of politics of convenience rather than principle and seeking to extend their control of the region, backed T'hami as suitably biddable and ruthless to ensure their smooth dominion. And if in the meantime he exploited that position for unfettered gain – what the hell!

According to Gavin Maxwell the elder brother Madani was 'ugly by any standards, but with a certain refinement of ugliness that excluded coarseness. With it he possessed a graciousness, an air of feline fastidiousness, that made his thin consumptive face with its enormous black velvet eyes and irregular yellow teeth one, according to early French writers, of "destiny and tragedy". Both he and his brother Thami were very dark skinned, but Thami was less positively ugly than his elder brother, less disdainful and enigmatic.'

It is said Thami was often charming and stylish and, as his wealth and power grew, many notable people including Charlie Chaplin, Winston Churchill and Maurice Ravel came to visit him.

Such charm did not extend to the treatment of his enemies. Returning from the coronation of Queen Elizabeth II of Great

Britain, he arranged for the heads of several dozen opponents to be mounted on the walls of his palace.

Thinking of leaders in my own time, old Thami was more an early representative of these mixing ruthlessness and charm to his own venal ends rather than being a throwback or relic of some more primitive past. Sure, I thought, Morocco has had more than its fair share of brutal and even psychopathic leaders, but most had some vision of an independent and vibrant state or a devout and religious society. Thami, it seems, was not troubled by such visions. As such he might be regarded as a very modern leader.

By mid-afternoon we had reached the outskirts of Ouarzazate. Here we stopped at a filling station with a café. It was next to some film studios – any film involving deserts or North African scenery seems to get shot in this region. I consumed two bottles of Sprite (cold but nauseous) two Solero ice-lollies, (perfect) and a Moroccan bitter lemon (challenging). I remember this detail because of the sheer orgasmic ecstasy of a cold drink on a wretched warm body.

Feeling somewhat restored, I could contemplate the daily ritual of the 'last twenty minutes' with equanimity, especially as it was through a beautiful oasis-like environment, around the river I could see we were heading towards. As we walked, Moha and I for once walking side-by-side, I suggested that we might spend the following night at a similar place to the accommodation at Ben Haddou, perhaps even again with a pool, anything to get cool, drink cool and recuperate cool. The alacrity with which he agreed suggested he too was feeling it, as we had now done nearly one hundred miles in five days. The idea proved to be prescient.

The twenty minutes turned out, not surprisingly, to be closer to two hours as we picked our way over riverbeds and the little fields and groves that characterise local agriculture.

Somehow we became separated from Muhammad, Hassan, the mules and Black and although we could phone them, as here we had phone signal, as neither party knew where they were arranging to rendezvous the communication veered between comic and exasperating.

Eventually we found them and started to build a camp a little way off the road on the edge of fields of alfalfa and under some trees. I sank down onto a mat, filthy, sweat-drenched, burned and incapable of any more. I must have fallen into a half sleep as after a while I became dimly aware of a sort of discussion going on around me in the space above my head. I looked through half-closed eyes to see a man in a blue T-shirt talking in a kind of busybody rapid way to Hassan, who was looking back at him defiantly. Muhammad, I noticed, was skulking around the edge the conversation. Black, more truthfully than me, was fast asleep and Moha was nowhere to be seen. Hassan had his phone in his hand and appeared to be ringing someone. Busybody did not stop his tirade of whatever, continuing to wave his arms and gesturing. I noticed a man in brown jacket was looking on. He looked grumpy and official, with an air of pompous certitude. He joined in and Hassan battled on.

The man in the blue T-shirt saw me and came over smiling and shook my hand. We tried an unsuccessful conversation in French but establishing mutual incomprehension he gave up and wandered back to Hassan who by now was involved in apoplectic debate with 'Mr Grumpy'. Muhammad looked at me, came over and hissed.

"Vous êtes très fatigué!"

Understanding that Muhammad wished to make me a difficult to move issue in the debate that seemed to have developed, I dutifully close my eyes and moderated my breathing to what I thought would indicate deep repose. By now a third person had turned up on an old spluttering moped, a huge guy in jeans and a black T-shirt, absolutely dwarfing the tiny machine on which he had arrived. At this point, Moha returned and the demonstrative handwaving, shoulder shrugging, gesticulating and face pulling resumed although I have to say that Moha was more reserved, maintaining a wry half smile on his face. Every so often everyone had to phone somebody, and people would move apart before returning to the ring and pointing to their phones as if the conversation they had just was written upon them.

I decided feigning sleep was not really contributing to situation and the fact I was taller and broader than everyone else except the big fellow might even things up psychologically a bit. I went over to join them.

"I guess they want us to move?" I asked.

"They are the local Caid's bureaucrats, and they don't understand anything," said Moha with exasperation. Caid is the general name for chief in these parts but more specifically the appointed head of the local community.

I stared at them crossly, which only provoked a recapitulation of the problem. So, Moha shrugged his shoulders and went and sat down on the stump of the tree.

Pointlessly I continued to glare at them whilst they talked amongst themselves. In the end I went and joined Moha.

"Looks like they have us!" I half joked, a touch of anxiety seasoning my curiosity as to where this was going to end.

"It is not a problem, Steve," Moha said in true laconic Berber style, ancestral centuries of defying would-be overlords rising up. "Either we stay here and there is no problem or we move to the hotel we are going to stay tomorrow, tonight and more no problem!"

"Unless we get arrested?"

Moha didn't answer.

By now the two guys had driven off in a dilapidated white car, leaving the big chap watching over us. Hassan decided to call the outcome and began dismantling the tent. Moha half-heartedly tried to remonstrate with him and then gave up.

"I guess we're going to jail or the hotel then?" I asked.

Moha said he just phoned up a guy we had met a few hours after the fuel stop. He had been driving a kind of three-wheeled motorbike and trailer loaded with large cans of olive oil and I had noticed Moha talking to him. I had thought nothing of it as Moha talks to everybody. But now he was going to come and pick us and our luggage up.

At that moment, the two men in their white car reappeared, joined by a uniformed and very small policeman who walked up to me apologetically and demanded papers.

So this was it! I was about to be detained, incarcerated even, for illegal camping. I decided to play dumb and the little French I had totally disappeared. The policeman took my passport and Moha's identity card and returned with them to the front of the car whilst the other two leaned in through the windows on the opposite side, instructing him and offering advice.

He wrote Moha's details on a torn piece of paper in pencil and then the pencil broke. The man in a blue T-shirt spoke to Moha who then returned to me grinning.

"He wants to know if you've got a pen he can borrow!"

This is not exactly carrying your own noose to the scaffold, but things did seem to be drifting in an unhelpful direction.

"Are we being arrested?" I asked Moha.

"I don't think so, not really, I'm not sure..."

So, I lent the policeman a pen and from somewhere they discovered they had a notebook and started to copy out pages and pages of my passport. The policeman sat in the passenger seat, Mr Grumpy in ostentatious outrage in the driver's seat.

In the meantime, the guy with the trike truck arrived. Soon, his little trailer was being loaded until it was piled high with our luggage, the mules being spared further exertion that day.

And then with a final flurry of conversation the policeman, Mr Blue T-shirt and Mr Grumpy climbed into the car, the big fellow put on his crash helmet and fired up his moped, and they all drove off into the evening.

We watched them go.

"Is that it?" I asked Moha.

"In Sha 'Allah," he said. "Anyway, we have a lift to the hotel – it's just up the road."

There was no obvious place to sit on the bike, since it had only one driver's seat, so I climbed onto the kind of document box bolted to the left hand side of the driver, put my feet on the mudguard in front and gripped the wooden frame behind me.

Moha climbed precariously on top of all the luggage.

"Lentement," I said, tapping the driver on his crash hat.

"Certainement," he replied as we accelerated viciously away, throwing a billowing cloud of dust up behind us.

It was a North African drive, bouncing over ruts in the road, swerving around near invisible pedestrians in the dusk, parting a sea of roller skaters, driving past a truck or several as we barrelled in through the outskirts of the town. At one time we seemed to be hurtling towards a huge crowd of people. As I hung on grimly, I was absolutely sure I would not be covered by my insurance if I fell or bounced off at any time but that if I died this way my children might be secretly rather proud of me.

Careering to a halt, we arrived at Les Jardins du Ouarzazate. It was a slightly battered old hotel with an air of faded charm. Equally charming staff welcomed us in, two of whom carried my bags to a room by an old swimming pool and turned on the chattering aircon for me. I went in feeling grateful to some guardian spirit that (a) I was not in a Moroccan jail, since they do not have the best of reputations, and (b) I was still alive and not crushed under a trike and a pile of dismembered roller-skaters.

Standing for a blissful time under a delinquent shower, which grumblingly offered me random blasts of cold and lukewarm water, I then got dressed and went to find some food. Moha and I reconvened on the hotel terrace to eat a little and to drink the slightly dodgy Moroccan wine that the hotel sold. Laughing at the adventures of the last few hours, I think we both were aware that this crazy trip had just moved up a gear and that the adventure had truly begun.

Chapter 7: The Krupp Cannon

Moha and I had agreed that this was going to be a rest day and that we would meet late afternoon and walk into town to visit the kasbah and see the famous cannon.

I settled down in shade by myself at breakfast and thought to myself what a blissful place this was. Les Jardins du Ourzazate is a medium-sized hotel on the outskirts of the town. The building itself is old and worn, cared-for but a bit run down in that charming Moroccan way that says don't throw something out just because it is a bit battered or threadbare. The patterned tiles, the old rug in the lobby, the doors and window frames, chairs by the pool were all shabby and well used. Even the menu reflected this, with a gentle hostility towards the unnecessary and the new reflected in an unchanging menu, which offered four starters, four main courses, printed on tatty card that must have been several years old. The triumph of the hotel was its gardens of poplar, pine, and palm together with clematis, geraniums and other brightly coloured flowers which I did not recognise, all competing for attention to the eye. There was a beautiful pool, slightly chipped in places but as clean as crisp linen.

There were very few guests in the hotel, since it was definitely late in the season, but I chatted for a while with a Canadian man who was travelling from the Sahara to the High Atlas Mountains, the opposite way to me. He was waiting for a guide to arrive at the hotel to work out which route they were going to take. He was only walking it in part but wanted a recommendation for a good mountain to walk up. Toubkal, I suggested – long, hard but do-able.

Apart from this brief encounter, I spent most of the day swimming, dozing and writing up my journal. We all needed some recuperation. On a patch of wasteland just outside the hotel, Black and the two mules snoozed under a tree in the mud and dirt. Inside the walled gardens under a shade, Muhammad and Hassan slept on long benches against a wall. When the heat of the day had receded a bit, they were going to wander into Ourzazate as well. Moha had told me that Hassan had some relatives in town whom they were going to visit.

Moha and I walked into the old town as finally the day started to dissipate some heat. Ouarzazate used to be a small crossing point for African traders making their way northern Morocco and Europe. The French, anxious to put their heel on the neck of the local population, had beefed it up as a garrison town and administrative centre. In the middle of it was the Kasbah of Taourirt, once owned by their faithful servant T'hami El Glaoui. It had been restored to some of its former glory and was the scene when we got there of some upmarket wedding or civil ceremony. Not that that deterred Moha, who in true Berber style, as I had discovered the previous night, did not easily bow his head to authority. And heading off purposefully we picked our way through a crowd, a film crew and some elegant looking people to find ourselves in front of the famous cannon in the corner of the courtyard.

So there it was! I am no connoisseur of the weapons of war, but it seemed quite small given its reputation and impact. I wondered what Madani and his brother might have achieved if they had been given one of the monstrous guns that would be produced for WW1 armies just a couple of decades later. It had a long steel muzzle, two wooden wheels with metal rim, two metal chairs, almost like ones you might find in an office, for the gunners at the back. It came with solid sturdy controls to adjust it and looked efficient, very German.

It was not the functional killing power of this gun that was its real potency but the fact that it was an object of almost spiritual reverence to Moroccans as a whole. In fact any cannon was cherished by Moroccans, Berber and Arab alike. Cannons were not just the symbol of the Sultan's temporal power but that of his spiritual authority as an Imam as well. It was believed that they could cure diseases, confer blessings, and grant asylum. They received offerings, often in the form of the decapitated heads of slain enemies, which were piled over and around them after a successful battle.

I gazed at it for a while, trying to imagine it being dragged through the snow by ill-clad soldiers as an icy wind blew and their comrades fell around them. But there was no call from the past, no real evocation of the tragedy and power of this instrument of destruction. To tell the truth it was a little disappointing, a piece of machinery, and like war itself, not glorious, just banal.

We looked around the rest of the Kasbah – it had been restored and, in a way, sterilised and it was hard to sense the way this place had dominated the surrounding region as a kind of mafiosi citadel for the Glaoui. For me, this Kasbah seemed to have surrendered its history by becoming a 'historical destination', compared with the lone, ruined kasbah bathed saffron in the evening mountain light we had found as we crossed the Atlas Mountains and down onto this high plateau.

Leaving the cannon to the chic and wealthy, Moha and I left the Kasbah and wandered into the Al-Mouahidine square in the middle of Ourzazate. We entered under a double-arched gateway as the sun began to set. The square was wide and well-maintained, paved with a geometric design and surrounded by low buildings containing shops and cafés. The buildings were of a yellowed umber and although traditional in style looked either new or well-maintained. Around them ran a low terrace, three steps above the main floor of the square on which sat, in groups of threes and fours, people old and young in deep convivial conversation. For this was the social hour, as the sun slipped away and people began to venture out. This scene was more timeless and redolent than anything the cannon could conjure up.

A stage had been erected in front of an official looking building and outside the succession of cafés on all sides of the square groups of men and families sat drinking coffee. Now and then local musicians would take to the stage and start to play, casting a mysterious musical spell over the sunset.

Moha stopped by a little stall selling *msemen*, a cross between a pancake and a flatbread which is fried so it is crispy on the outside. Berbers eat it with honey and jam for breakfast; or on its own or with vegetables or mincemeat later in the day. We sat and ate a couple, drinking half-decent coffee, listening to the music, people-watching and talking.

Ourzazate has more dark-skinned people than I saw up in the Atlas Mountains. Many would have been descended from the slaves which the Berber tribes had kept in large numbers until well into the twentieth century. The relationship between the slaves and the Berbers was more complex than in other examples of this awful trade. The mother of Madani and T'hami Glaoui was Zouhra Oum El Khaïr, a black slave. This ancestry was no inhibition to their status and advancement. According to the already-mentioned intrepid Dr Rohlfs, a German doctor who travelled through Morocco in the mid 19th Century cautiously dressed as an Arab, slaves were brought here from Timbuktu having been purchased in the Sudan, 'at the cheap price of from two to three pounds; although young, pretty and fair-complexioned. They are then resold in Fez and Morocco (Marrakech) at a considerable profit, fetching from 15 to 25 pounds each.'

If this is true, slaves from the Sudan would have already travelled over 2000 miles to Timbuktu before they embarked on the final Saharan crossing into Morocco.

Although slaves were the absolute property of their owners, to be used and abused as they pleased, they were, according to Gavin Maxwell, an integral part of a household who 'enjoyed a degree of protection and security considerably greater than the average freeman. Favourite slaves, freed slaves often rose to positions of great power.'

This probably says more about the condition in which ordinary Moroccans lived than anything at all positive about slavery. Black slaves also made up for centuries the elite Black Guard of the Moroccan army, reporting only to the Sultan. As a source of enormous power in the country they could engineer the rise and fall of even the most powerful.

Sitting convivially listening to the music, by now a unison of chanting, a tuned bass stringed instrument, tuned drums and a percussive rattle, Moha remarked thoughtfully that this was the sound of castanets. They came to North Africa and were said to the imitate the clinking of the slaves' chains as they walked along. I suddenly realised the music I was listening was probably Gnawa – the hypnotic, transcendental music of the enslaved Africans who used it to connect themselves to their ancestors and to heal people possessed by genie spirits. This music has become popular not just in North Africa but amongst the global roots music community; but here in the market square where most likely slaves were bought and sold, here was to glimpse through to another place, far in terms of distance, story and memory from my own. This was a confluence point for streams and rivers of humanity and stories of which I knew myself to be profoundly ignorant.

I began to see Moha as the go-between from my own solitary experience and the rich and mysterious universe of which, in this moment, in this way, I was a solitary alien. This, I suddenly thought, was profoundly different to the normal experience packaged into the tourist experience. Although an alien, I felt a connection to something I could not understand.

And this sense of dislocation and intrigue was heightened as Moha explained that the large ensemble of musicians were now drumming and dancing a kind of performance called Ahwash, which may have come from Telouet. Predating the coming of Islam, but now interwoven uneasily with it, Ahwash speaks to the supernatural and may gift its performers with clairvoyance.

Moha then returned to the topic of the Jewish people who had once lived here. The amiability that once existed between Moslems and Jews in this region was something he felt represented some important quality of the Berber people. He seemed haunted by it.

"There are many different peoples that came here," he said, "and there was understanding."

Moroccan Jews were the largest of Jewish communities in North Africa, about 250,000 people, who made up one tenth of the total population after the Second World War. Most of them left following Moroccan independence and the establishment of the state of Israel. Afraid of the growing polarisation and enmity between Arab and Jew, they looked for safety and in doing so felt forced to abandon their homes, their language, their culture and their sense of identity.

They had lived here for thousands of years and spoke Berber, living in distinct but integrated neighbourhoods, called mellahs, within the larger community. Now there are only 5,000 Jewish Moroccans left in the whole of Morocco and these mellahs are abandoned and almost, but not totally, forgotten. This old relationship between Moslem and Jew was poignantly explored by French-Moroccan director, Kamal Hachkar in his award-winning documentary *Tinghir-Jerusalem: Echoes from the Mellah.*

Tinghir, Moha told me, is about 100km north of here and all the Jewish people had left in the 1960s.

"It is great film – it brings people together – they showed it at a special screening in Tinghir, people were very emotional," said Moha.

Kamal Hachkar was born in Tinghir himself to a Moslem family before moving to France. In one scene he arranges an on-line meeting between his father, who has gone back to Tinghir to live, and Shalom Ilouz, a Berber-speaking Jew who now lives in Israel. Shalom remembers Kamal's grandfather, who had a silk shop in Tinghir.

In an emotional conversation as Kamal's father excitedly tells Shalom:

"This is your country here!"

Together they search for mutual friends: Sidi Bouxa's children; Ilou, who ran the coach company; Mimou, a tourist guide; Moshe Hanina who owned the café; Lhacen N'Ait Kadi, the tailor and artisan Daoud, who Shalom used to work for.

Shalom sadly observes:

"I always think about the village and its people. The village Moslems were very good people."

Although radical groups in the Arab and Moroccan world accused Kamal Hachkar of being 'pro-Zionist' and wanting to 'normalise relations with Israel', most ordinary Moroccans were more welcoming of the documentary,

Rachid Khouya, a staff writer on Moroccan World News (2013) wrote about the screening:

They carried with them the names of their friends, the songs of mothers and the tales of grandmothers. They still bear inside the languages of the ancestors. They hang on their walls musical instruments of the mountains and they sing and dance songs of love and nostalgia to the days when the people of the same village, both Muslims and Jews, lived side by side and danced in ceremonies side by side and when people of both religions stood as a strong soldier to defend the villages and their people from the attacks of enemies and neighbouring tribes.

People have been bound together in this place from all over central and eastern Africa, as slaves, as merchants, as adventurers, as invaders – so many different sorts of people. Peoples who have been largely forgotten by history or disappeared altogether, stirred into a whole, in which people could say others were part of themselves.

And perhaps it is the idea of tolerance, community and companionship and the culture that evolves that builds a sense of identity? It is not just genetics, for there seems to be no particular genetic code that says this person is or is not Berber.

According to my own DNA profile, through my mother's line I share 61% of my DNA with the Tuareg (a Berber tribe), but that does not make me of this place or give me the right to claim these as my people.

Rachid Khouya goes on to write:

Personally, as a Moroccan who is Amazigh, Muslim, who speaks Tamazight, and Arabic and who has grown up in the Sahara, I am so proud of this diversity which allowed me to drink from different cultural springs and sources (Amazigh, Arabic, Sahara, Muslim and African.) I consider this a special Moroccan gift that makes our cultural and national richness and unity.

And finally, as we headed back to Les Jardins du Ourzazate, I wondered, in the warp and weft of humanity that had gathered in this marketplace, how it might be possible to lose or hide a tribe of dwarfs.

Chapter 8: Walking on the Moon

The following day we set off reasonably early: Moha, Muhammad, Hassan, Black and me. And of course, the blessed mules. If ever a creature was maligned with the word 'stubborn' it is a mule. Contemplative, patient, strong, sure-footed: any of these words would be more appropriate and honourable. The Berbers do not gift their beasts with names but the attention and care they received, particularly from Muhammad who at every stop unburdened and fed them before turning to his own needs, suggests a relationship more than transactional. The amount they seem to happily carry always astonishes me.

Crossing the rest of the high plain and up and across the Anti-Atlas Mountains was tough. There are no paths or routes across the desert, and up over the blasted mountains and following the single road that wound its way from the plains and over the top would have been much, much longer, and tedious. Instead, we decided to take a more direct route, rejoining the road now and then as it switched back and forward. Muhammad, Hassan, Black and the mules would join us either when we used the road or when the cross country going was smooth enough for the mules. We saw hardly anyone else; the mountains are too arid and desolate to support much in the way of life and the only humankind we saw was after a couple of days, when the occasional overburdened truck ground its way up to where some road construction was going on, with one or two workers who struggled away in the blistering heat.

Out of Ourzazate we walked for a while along the road. It was already ridiculously hot and dusty. It would have been extremely easy to say, "just one more day!" However, a stiff breeze offered some cooling action and after a couple of hours Moha and I dropped into the shade of a Wadi, on the sides of which a couple of palm trees offered some shade. Moha smoked a cigarette. I noticed he always politely removed himself a few metres to smoke. The last few days he had had an ongoing cough. I felt I knew him well enough by now to point out that the regular intake of Gauloise cigarettes and the coughing may be related. He ruefully agreed and said he intended to stop but that cigarettes were part of the way people got on in Morocco, and people freely asked and were given them.

We ate lunch on the banks of the nearly dried-up river. The gusting wind kept the heat manageable. Black rested at my feet as we lay recuperating and eating a salad with spicy cooked lentils prepared by Hassan. I liked the fact that when Hassan and Muhammad stopped it always felt as if we had truly taken some time to pause. Unlike back at home where every moment seemed to be being dragged to a hasty conclusion by the demands to 'get on' with the next obligation, here time was not the driver. We stopped, the mules were unpacked and Hassan and Muhammad set stuff down carefully. They then untethered the mules and left them to wander. Then, as always, salad was prepared, Hassan squatting on the ground carefully chopping ingredients on an old tray. The rickety stove was lit, and some beans cooked, and the mint tea made with reverence. As usual it was at least half an hour before any food appeared. I smiled at the thought of the friends back home who might be driven insane by this. The meal was eaten slowly, punctuated by conversation and cigarettes. Moha, crouching on his haunches with the other two chatted in Berber, whilst I, a little way away, letting my bare feet breathe in the air, communed with Black. I loved these moments on our trek, with an open-ended sense of time. There was a time to walk and a time to recover, to observe and reflect, a time to suffer and a time to rejoice. A feeling that we would get somewhere when we did. A kind of Ecclesiastes, reduced.

Then, dishes and crockery cleaned, everything carefully repacked, and the mules reloaded, we set off again. We soon left the road and started to cross the Anti-Atlas Mountains. After an initial ascent and cresting a ridge, it seemed as if I was in an endless broken moonscape of cracked rock. An enormous flat plateau of boulders stretched to a far horizon where occasional peaks, almost pyramidical alien structures, stood witness to the desolation. Later the landscape became fissured as if some enormous grim hand with iron nails had dragged their fingers through the rock and the earth to create canyons and escarpments and twisted valleys, sometimes squeezing the fierce rock till despite itself, it folded and bent. From the top of one ridge, I looked, and the same bleak and baked landscape seemed to stretch on forever.

The terrain meant that the going was very tough, the way strewn with large boulders and broken stones that meant measuring and placing every stride on the uneven and unpredictable surface. Moving was a slow, messy business.

As we climbed up the side of one steep, rubble-strewn slope, Moha, who was of course a little ahead of me, suddenly stopped and, waving his arm deliberately up-and-down, signalled for me to do the same. He seemed to stand for a while staring at something ahead of him, but I could not work out what it was. He then stooped down and picked up a stone and threw it in front of him. The next thing I knew a long thin snake reared up in front of him in a kind of S shape and lunged. The snake missed Moha and decided to make a bolt for it, straight towards me. Moha waved for me to move towards him or away, I could not tell which, but strict instructions given on a previous trip to Namibia kicked in and instead I stood very still, and the snake slid away to one side of me.

"That was interesting," said Moha, "I thought it was dead, but I threw a stone just in case. It must have been a juvenile or it wouldn't have missed!"

That night we met up with the others and camped on a piece of flat ground on a high rocky plateau, from which the mountain fell away on both sides. Not far away was a deserted camp for construction workers building a new road through the mountains. Incongruously, and presumably for the road workers, a deep well had been dug at the edge of the flat ground. An old rubber bucket tied to a rope sat on the round wall that encircled it. We wound the old bucket down and back up again. It was now filled with the most wonderous pure, cool water which we poured over our heads, letting the water run down, soaking our clothes and our shoes.

I gave some to Black and scooped more up and wetted his head and shoulders - he looked at me with appreciation.

Sitting on a rock I let that wonderful feeling of 'a day's work done' seep over me. I looked around at this barren pitch and the abandoned workers huts gathered at a distance like an old Mexican ghost town and knew that I felt happy. 'This is wilderness,' I thought, 'This is where the most likely thing to meet is yourself.'

It was late, getting dark, as we pitched our tents and I watched Muhammad and Hassan struggling with the big poles and creaking canvas of their tent as it was tossed about in a particularly fierce and gusting wind. I saw no point in wasting time with the flimsy thing I had been given, which seemed to be made of a second cousin to Chinese paper and decided to sleep outside under the night sky, something which I did the rest of the trip. I created a sort of open sarcophagus with bags placed around a sleeping mat to keep the worst of the dust off and, still feeling unable and not needing to eat, lay down to sleep. Black came over to inspect me, tilting his head to one side quizzically as if thinking,

"So, you're not allowed inside either?"

I patted his head, and he turned his big brown eyes towards me and stared into mine.

"We are both a long way from home," he seemed to be thinking.

"Home is where the heart is," I said aloud, remembering an old lyric.

I could not help thinking Black understood.

He lifted a paw slightly and then turned and not far away circled round in the grit and dust and settled down to sleep. I did the same. I looked for my old iPod, intending to stare at the stars and listen to some music to ease into slumber as I lay in my open tomb. There was no sound except some snoring from the tent next to me and the gentle stiff flap of the old canvas in the wind. The bustle of Ouarzazate already seemed a million miles away. I wondered whether the camel trains winding their way over this terrain, with swaying camels and shuffling slaves, had ever stopped for the night here. That well was older than it appeared. I tried to imagine a hundred or so camels hunkered down on this plain, relieved of their saddles and bags which were piled, as if sleeping, around them. A fire would be lit, and people would be talking softly, staring into the flames and conjuring images of the Kasbah and the coffee and mehmets in the Al-Mouahidine square they might reach the following day.

Just on the threshold of sleep, Black startled me suddenly by scrambling to his feet and barking once very loudly and menacingly and then continuing to growl in a low menacing way. There was an answering challenge from the darkness and a call and response of threat and counter threat ensued as a pack of wild dogs prowled around in the gloom not so far away. I think they were originally attracted to this remote place by the deserted camp a little distance away. In the twilight and darkness, they circled around our little refuge. I wondered if Moha and the others were aware of them, but all was silent in the old square tent.

Black sat bolt upright, seemingly on guard and I settled on top of my sleeping bag, bush knife at my side and tried to remember my friend Ben McNutt's instructions for killing coyotes. Every so often Black, presumably deciding the pack were getting too close, would charge off into the darkness and there would be a sharp bark, even a yelp and he would calmly reappear, sitting upright while checking things were under control, before lying down again and slipping into watchful sleep.

I remembered reading about the diplomat, explorer, author, soldier and former politician Rory Stewart's account of walking 750km across Afghanistan in 36 days. Near the start of this he was offered a dog to accompany him on his journey, which he, with some reluctance, accepted. He called him Babur which means tiger.

He had been a fighting dog for the locals but had suffered loss of teeth and had had his ears cut off. But he had a head like a bear and an air of imperturbability which he shared with Black.

Rory Stewart undertook this walk just after the fall of the first Taliban regime when the country was still riven, violent and very, very dangerous. His relationship with the dog was deep and spontaneous. At one level it made no sense but at another it was deep and mutual. Who was looking after whom was never certain. At one time Stewart is exhausted, alone and sitting in the snow at that point where it is easier to and more comfortable to let go of life than struggle on. The dog came over to him and Stewart says:

I could feel his warm breath on my neck as he sniffed carefully around my collar and gently pushed his nose against my ear. When I did not respond he backed away, watched me, approached again and finally began to walk away across the snow plain, occasionally looking over his shoulder. When he was 200 yards ahead he stopped, turned and barked once. His matter-of-fact just made me feel that I was being melodramatic. If he was going to continue, so was I. I stood up and followed his tracks.

I looked at Black, strong, conditionally faithful, carrying his adventures upon himself with assurance. Like Babur, I reflected that he was meant to be here, part of the hidden tug of the journey. He surely is a 'spirit dog', I reflected to myself. There was an aura of protection and guardianship about him, as if he was looking after us more than himself.

I stared up into the vast bowl of heaven, feeling as whole as I ever have done. The breeze had died down, the wild pack of dogs had given up their attempt at a raid, and Black would ensure that we all would have a night of calm and restoration.

For a while the wind died and this spot on earth hushed. Sleeping wild over the years, I have come to know that the wilderness is rarely as silent as you might imagine. In the forests of Appalachia, you are sung to sleep by a chorus of randy frogs and lustful cicadas; on the frozen winter lakes of Ontario the ice creaks and snow plummets with a dull whoosh from the trees; and in New Mexico, coyotes indulge in Evensong. But there, all then became silent. Another sort of emptiness. In it I thought I might hear the sound of the stars.

Chapter 9: The Badlands

Later that night the wind blew up and continued long and hard and I didn't sleep that well. But that was fine. A billion stars or more stretched from horizon to horizon and despite the low murmuring of the sleeping gang in the tent opposite I felt comfortably alone.

Untethered, as if I was floating free from the web of my past, I sensed being opened to unfolding possibility.

I woke up to the last gasp of seeming cool before the sun crested the mountainous horizon and the heat began to rapidly climb. Moha as usual was sitting on a rock a little way away smoking. Black was sitting convivially next to him. It almost seemed as if they were in conversation.

I looked around to see more clearly where I was in the fresh light of a new day. A flat rocky plateau, a well, and some distance away the empty workers' huts and a few sharp thorn bushes. All was as before.

If there is a place called nowhere, I decided this might be it. I was tired and I knew it. And I was struggling to keep hydrated and had scarcely eaten since we had left Ourzazate.

Back on our way, the terrain continued as the same blasted wilderness as the previous days, with the temperature relentlessly rising. We picked our way over rocks, stumbled over low gulleys, zig-zagged down steep slopes. We moved in silence, even the mules seeming to focus on their footing.

The sense of low-level bliss in which I had awoken soon dissipated and after a few hours I was struggling with the overwhelming feeling that internally and externally I was too hot. My mouth was caked with a thick sticky mucus, and I couldn't swallow properly. My lips got stuck together and sipping on the more than lukewarm water in my bottle seemed to make little difference. I became desperate to swallow something cold.

By late that afternoon, the heat and the effort of walking on a ground where you could never hit your stride was really taking its toll and I was literally forcing myself to put one foot in front of another. I became very disoriented and started to violently retch now and again.

Feeling as much as anything foolish and frustrated, I ground to halt and sat against the broken and forgotten wall of an abandoned goat enclosure, incapable of any further movement. Moha was out of sight much further ahead. In a small depression in the ground, I saw a bright blue chameleon looking at me, its colour making it as much out of place as I felt. I sat back and pondered what to do next. Sitting here wasn't an option but I couldn't think of anything else. I forced myself to drink most of the rest of the water I was carrying, pathetically pouring the remainder over my head to enjoy the momentary cooling effect.

For the first time, I felt certain I wouldn't make it. It was too hard, too far, too hot. I castigated myself for the foolishness of having believed that I could. The very idea of getting to my feet overwhelmed me. I started to wonder how I could explain to the world, indeed to myself, what had gone wrong.

After about twenty minutes Moha returned, looking anxious.

"Are you okay?" he asked.

"No," I replied, "but I know I need to keep going." I staggered on another couple of miles until on the other side of a low valley I could see a low line of buildings along the horizon, the outskirts of Ait Saouin, a village on the road that passes through the Anti-Atlas. The first habitation since we had a left Ourzazate and one that Moha thought might have a street café or shop with a refrigerator that sold cold drinks.

I counted out my paces in blocks of a hundred, then would stand for a minute to sip some water and press on. Moha was clearly anxious about the state I was in. He offered to go on ahead and send one of the mules back, but that would have lengthened the journey even more and by now I was completely desperate just to get out of the heat.

Eventually, still stumbling and retching, I followed Moha through the outskirts of the village. This consisted of empty mudbrick buildings in various states of repair. In my ruined state I began to think the place had been abandoned but minutes later I staggered into little place with a cane awning outside under which men, faces etched by the sun, sat smoking and drinking glasses of mint tea. They regarded me with complete indifference. Inside it was more or less empty, but did have a fridge containing a few cans of soft drinks.

I felt very, very ill. Miraculously, I found that my phone had a signal and I called my daughter Samantha, who is a doctor. Sounding very worried, she told me to drink very slowly, preferably flat sugary drinks and take my time.

I sat at a rickety table and drank my way gradually and deliberately through sickly sweet cans of fizzy orange and apple juice and began to feel less desperate. Moha's offer of Berber whisky (hot, sweet mint tea) I politely turned down.

That night, Moha persuaded me to eat a little spaghetti and some tinned fruit, my first food for 36 hours. The tinned fruit especially tasted wondrous. Still finding myself incapable of a coherent sentence, I soon gave up trying to be sociable and slept outside again. For several semi-conscious hours I lay on a ground mat in a bittersweet reverie thinking about, and sometimes talking to, my long dead mother.

Black once again kept guard. Two packs of dogs stalked the camp, grumbling and occasionally fighting with each other. Sometimes when Black was chasing one off the other would get close. I woke once to see two or three mean looking beasts about twenty feet away from the camp tent. I sat up and threw stones at them until Black hurtled out of the darkness and drove them away.

Again I saw how Black had become so much more than an opportunistic scavenger hitching along for the ride. On the road he tagged along a few metres away from us but always seemed to be keeping watch, not that he was particularly road wise. I had several panicky moments on the short sections when we walked along the road and he would sit down for a scratch as an overburdened watermelon lorry hurtled towards him. Muhammad had no sense of ownership, and I don't think it occurred to him to do much in the way of care. The rest of us were becoming more involved though. I had taken it upon myself to fashion him a drinking bowl by cutting up an old plastic water bottle. Hassan also seemed to be growing fond of the dog, but it was Moha with whom he had really started to bond. When we had stopped that lunchtime Black had, as usual, come up and sniffed and wagged his tail to Muhammad, Hassan and me, putting his beautiful wise head to one side as if to check we were okay. To Moha, however, he jumped up as if trying to hug to him and Moha, with delight, responded, tickling his ears, and laughing at him.

The next day I rode on a mule for the first hour. I was still feeling groggy, and we were facing a steep ascent up a long road. I fought against feelings that somehow, I was cheating (cheating what?) to ride on a mule – that I would no longer be technically walking *all* the way. It is funny how a story can capture you. 'Walking all the way' was, I guess, an implied rather than conscious expectation, but so many people had incredulously asked me before I left:

"Are you going to walk *all* the way?"

I had somehow become infected with the notion I should do so.

That day, unlike the previous day, we were walking along a recently metalled, twisting road where walking was much easier. But the road had its own trials in the shape of overburdened coughing trucks, loaded to the skies with watermelons, grinding up towards us. Black caused Moha and me palpitations when, oblivious to their approach, he wandered back and forward between the narrow carriageway and the vertiginous drop on one side of the road. Or sat down to have a scratch.

This truly was the badlands: wilderness and wildness. Only the desperate and the mad, I thought, would want to live here. For the laden camel trains crossing here as they made their way into or out of the Sahara, this must have sometimes been a very grim challenge. By now there was virtually no vegetation except for occasional cruel, sharp thorn bushes that remained, refusing to die. Earlier and sparsely there had been argan bushes and sage and – astonishingly defiant – little groups of palm trees now and then beside an abandoned and broken mud house.

Notwithstanding the harshness, there was a forbidding beauty here. The first day had been a flat, alien, bouldered plain edged by monolithic pinnacles of really weathered rock, buttes and what they call in the States hoodoos. Occasionally the shadow of one would cross the plain, providing moments of shade to be traded for the efforts of crossing them. The previous day, for our midday stop I had lain dozing in the 30cm shadow cast by an overhanging rock.

Today, as we headed up the pass this scene gave way to canyons and swirling, deep, multi-coloured valleys. As with the mineral hues of the High Atlas, there was something surreal and dreamlike about the colours.

This was a land created in a very distant past, at the near beginning of things, to the height or more than the Himalayas when two giant supercontinents collided. At one time, in the resulting supercontinent of Pangea, sharp-toothed dinosaurs would have roamed.

I guess I rode the mule for about half an hour before anxiety over Black's road sense, or lack of it, plus my pride and foolishness, forced me to get off. Twenty-two miles later, having crossed the Anti-Atlas Mountains, we arrived at the outskirts of Agdz.

We stopped for a drink in a roadside café. We were all exhausted. The goal was to get to the other side of Agdz. Moha's strategy was always to rest up on the far side of any bigger settlement and we all quietly suspected we were in for a another of Moha's two-hour 'twenty minutes'. The thought meant we sat in silence.

Moha and I set off first. Muhammad and Hassan returned to the mules to reload, and riding them with Black trotting alongside, we knew they would soon catch up with us.

The streets on the edge of town seemed roughly a grid iron shape. People loitered in the shade of doorways, little shops without a front wall or door opened on to the road selling car tyres, plastic buckets, sacks of flour and cans of cooking oil. Children played football in the rough street. Now and then a mule accompanied by a youth in jeans and a T-shirt or a wizened old guy with a djellaba would trot past. Downtown North Africa.

After about fifteen minutes of walking, the others joined us: the two mules, Mohammad, and Hassan.

But no Black.

Moha spotted his absence first.

"Where is Black?" he asked in English and then in Berber.

Muhammad shrugged his shoulders. Hassan looked upset. And a brief and animated conversation ensued between Hassan and Moha, who eventually turned to me and explained.

"When they got to the outskirts of the town by the busy road he simply stopped and wouldn't come any further. They pressed on expecting him to follow but he did not."

"Didn't they go and look for him?" I asked. I felt a tone of accusation in my voice which Moha sensed.

"I am sure he will track us down," he said, "otherwise we will go back and look for him in the morning."

I couldn't help but think this was wishful thinking. We walked on in silence. Even Muhammad seemed uncomfortable.

Again Moha's twenty minutes turned into two very long hours. We pressed on out of town and, crossing a river, made our way along the winding riverside to where we were going to stay that night. As we crossed the bridge, I saw two boys fishing in the ponds that remained where the river had flowed earlier in the year. One of them caught quite a large fish in a relatively small pond. I don't suppose the pond was more than 3 metres long. It didn't seem fair somehow.

That day we walked over 24 miles. All in all we had done over 145 miles. Perhaps it was this that introduced the sense of tetchiness amongst us. The last few days had been very hard, and I knew that particularly Hassan had been concerned about the terrain, the distance, and the impact on the mules. A perfectly understandable reaction, given that the two mules constituted a precarious means of making a living. Perhaps it was just being so far from home. Neither he nor Muhammad had really left the Atlas Mountains before, and this was by far the furthest into the desert they had ever gone.

As the weary and sombre miles went on and it began to grow dark, Hassan was walking along side me leading a mule.

He was muttering to himself in French, "trop loin, trop loin." Too far, too far.

"Une longue journée", I sympathised.

Hassan looked at me. "Black dix, Moha zero!" he said.

And then repeated it.

I think until that moment I had seen this trek selfishly through my own eyes. I had not really thought about the distance, the time away from home for these guys who would normally be involved in treks of a couple of days, never more than a week. Sure, my relationship with them had been cheerful and playful – they found my inability to pronounce Berber words a source of great amusement and I think Hassan secretly appreciated that I would tease Muhammad about which of us was older (he was over 70).

But the truth was I had let them slip into being bit players in my world, minor characters in my story rather than opening my heart and mind to who they really were. This was their adventure as well and I resolved to remember it.

Eventually, as dusk fell, we arrived at the Kasbah Ilrine near the village and great fortress of Tamnougalt. The Kasbah was a kind of Berber guest house with a shaded area outside around a cracked and chipped, but clean, pool. Inside were big, high-ceilinged, gloomy rooms sweltered in time, although the bedrooms had rattling but effective air con units. I ate on my own. A rare selfie I took that evening shows a very battered, disreputable looking chap with batty professor hair and a mad look in his eyes.

Moha came by briefly. He didn't argue when I said I thought we were all done in. I said I thought the guys were fed up and he didn't argue with that either. He just looked back quietly. And the realisation of my own narrow selfish focus hit me again. I hadn't really considered the pressure as well on Moha. It's not as if we were following a defined trek with an ordered set of stopping points, perhaps with a detailed guide, almost an instruction manual, as you would find with the routes in America or the UK. As far as either of us knew no one else had tried to take this journey on foot and particularly at this time of year. This whole mad enterprise in getting this Englishman with a dodgy knee more than three hundred miles at pace across mostly desert, plus keeping Muhammed and Hassan, who were probably getting way outside their geographic comfort zone, on side must have been a terrific strain as well.

I was determined to be more mindful of the rest of the team. We agreed to spend another day here and use tomorrow to recuperate. I gave Moha some cash for the guys to take some time out – I felt embarrassed about doing this, afraid of being a typical wealthy westerner doing the *noblesse oblige* bit, but then again it was a practical and meaningful thing to do. Moha took the money and said they would appreciate it. He said tomorrow we should all have a good rest, and he would go into Agdz and look for Black.

By the following evening it was clear: Black was gone.

It was almost as if he had seen us all safely to the large settlement and felt he had done his bit. I cannot lie: I felt his loss, and in the strangest of ways I still do. It's not as if I hadn't had great faithful dogs who had lived and been loved and died. But this felt like something else. The next day, benefiting from a rare internet connection, I wrote a long Facebook post to update friends and sponsors on the crossing of the Anti-Atlas and mentioned the disappearance of Black. The internet crackled into life, people asking for answers on his whereabouts, offering to look after him, wanting him flown to England. Clearly, he had won many hearts. Several had stories of dogs that had adopted them in similar circumstances.

A huge drum major from an Australian Pipe and Drum band wrote to me about 'a mighty hound of salvation!'

My old friend Lewis - art gallery director and adventurer – reminded me of the Rory Stewart story.

Another of being joined by a dog that was a guide and defender across Crete.

A behavioural scientist would probably reduce this whole episode to a kind of trade – man provides dog with rather ropey supply of food, dog provides man with unrealistic sense of security, physical and perhaps even emotional. That is the way of the pseudo-rational because you cannot meaningfully reduce a relationship to a sum of transactions. They just won't divide up like that. Black was representative of a truth as old as we are - that we travel best with companions. In any wilderness we flourish because of those we travel with. It can be part of freedom's gift that we do not have to travel alone.

I can't help believing, or even perhaps wanting to believe, that Black was something more and in a way that is part of the reality. In my mind Black saw us out of the desert, saw that we were safe and moved on. And that is how I choose to remember him. He surely was a 'spirit dog', I thought to myself. There was an aura of protection and guardianship about him, as if he were looking after us more than the other way round. Native Americans have long believed in the notion of a spirit dog as something that would provide security, unconditional love, and, most important, loyalty. Many stories tell that those who mistreated dogs were to be severely punished, while those who showed kindness would gain the favour of the Great Spirit.

Chapter 10: Stumbling Over Eden

Twelve days into the adventure, leaving the Kasbah Ilrine, we walked past the great fortress of Tamnougalt, its huge weary brown walls quiet and brooding. There was a kind of peaceful melancholy about the place. Probably about 200 years old, it is impressive and forgotten, though according to Moha within its crumbling walls one or two members of the old family linger on.

The history of Tamnougalt is ancient. It is intimately tied up with its situation close to the Mezguita oasis, one of the six situated on the Draa river flowing out from the Atlas Mountains. The Draa is Morocco's longest river, at 1,100 kilometres. It runs from the Atlas Mountains, initially south-eastward along the edge of the range before turning back on itself and heading west at Tagounite to its mouth in the Atlantic Ocean. The river valley is fertile and providential, providing irrigation and a means of to life in a desolate wasteland. Bounded to the West by the Atlas Mountains and to the east and south and even north by the Sahara, this has never been an easy place to get to, which may account for it being the cradle of Berber rebelliousness and independence.

For centuries the sons of Taleb el Hassan ruled here as the Caid, a Berber overlord, in an uneasy relationship with their neighbours the Glaoui further up the valley. It was a relationship in which nominal alliances were often disrupted by greedy eyes. In this case the grass *was* always greener. Maintaining the family tradition, Thami led a 'harka'to Tamnougalt in 1919. The best way to think about a harka is as an armed tax-collecting expedition. Then in 1923 his cousin Hammou advanced on the place, attacking the village with more than 5,000 men and their favourite Krupp cannon. The siege lasted 17 days before the inhabitants surrendered.

It is said that even by the Glaoui families' bloody standards, Hammou was something else. Referred to as 'the Vulture', he was known for his sadism. He was particularly fond of throwing random and innocent people into dark dungeons and simply forgetting about them. As with other Moroccan potentates, fear built up by his arbitrary cruelty was his primary source of power as a leader.

Attacking a dissident kasbah near Telouet itself, he burned it down, roasting alive everyone inside including the women and children. As Thami became more anxious to be accepted by the French authorities and to hang out with the great and the good, Hammou became one of those embarrassing relatives that you feel you have to invite to important events but rather hope they don't turn up.

Walking along with the wall of the fortress to our left, to our right were narrow entrances in shoulder-high mud walls. Turning into one, we found ourselves in a maze of paths over which towered tall palm trees, under which lay a scene of almost inexpressible beauty.

In the flickering light, pomegranate, almond, apricot and fig trees grew around little walled patches of graceful wheat, barley and alfalfa. Their fruit hung to be picked as if offering themselves. Tamarind trees, their thin blue leaves pointing upwards like brushes, guarded the little groves and fields where patient women carefully tended their crops. Birds sang and frogs croaked in the little irrigation ditches and streams that wove their way through this glimpse of paradise. After the harshness of the Anti-Atlas Mountains, it felt like I was stumbling over Eden itself. In the twinkling shade of the trees, I sat upon the ground and let myself be overwhelmed by the sense of abundance that grew all around me: in the murmuring of insects, in the low voices of the women working in the fields, in the scent of blossom and fruit, and in the touch of a breeze and the dabbling light.

After the trials of the trek so far, the excessive heat, the distance, the loss of Black and – as I dwelt upon it – the pointless grind of much of my existence, this spot murmured:

"Let go. Let go of these trials."

What astonishment and delight it would have offered the sand-beaten traveller arriving here after their very existence had been questioned as they crossed the desert ocean. A sudden vision of plenty and ease.

I guess I had always thought about Eden in biblical terms, the garden of God in Genesis and also the book of Ezekiel. But its story is older than that and the writing of it in the Bible. Scholars say it echoes Mesopotamian myths about guarding the tree of life. Some people have tried to locate the garden in various places in the Persian Gulf, in Iraq, Iran or in the Armenian high lands.

Eden is one of the most ancient myths that stories from the beginnings of consciousness are woven into. The tree, the serpent, the fruit, even Adam and Eve lie in our shared memory before the writing of the Bible. According to Arthur George and Elaina George in their weighty book *The Mythology of Eden*, the biblical story developed from different sources and these sources contributed to the somewhat conflicting narrative that we find in the Bible today.

In a much earlier version of the story of Adam, Eve was his second wife. The first, Lilith, was a colourful character who apparently would not subordinate herself to Adam and would not have sex with him unless she was on top. Eventually she abandoned him, leaving the stage open for Eve to be created from Adam's rib.

This is not to debunk the story but to celebrate its fundamental message for our sense of identity. Perhaps Eden is really a state of mind. Not a myth, not some archaeological remnant, but an expression of hope for the weary traveller through life. It is a place where in the hardships of the wilderness we can imagine our physical and spiritual needs are met. A place where one day we can hope to let go of the trials of the road. It is a sanctuary; it is the manifestation of the sublime. It is a deep universal sense of home.

As the poet Kathleen Raine wrote in *Message from Home*:

Man, with farther to travel from his simplicity,
from the archaic moss, fish, and lily parts,
and into exile travels his long way.

At that moment, as I sat there, I felt in touch with something that makes the lonely traveller roam, ironically to find that part of themselves that, because of where and how they live, they have lost.

As you leave Eden behind you, remember your home,
For as you remember back into your own being
You will not be alone; the first to greet you
Will be those children playing by the burn,
The otters will swim up to you in the bay,
The wild deer on the moor will run beside you.[6]

Every so often through the trees I could see the severe cliff faces, the valley sides and the slopes of humped Jbel Kissane towering over us in its strange pastel colours to remind me I was in a sanctuary.

Shaking myself from my reverie I rose and hurried to catch up with Moha. Emerging from the trees, we walked alongside the Draa River on the opposite bank, peaceful with bamboo and palm trees. By now we had reached a level of very companionable conviviality, chattering away as we strolled along or as we sat for a while in the cracked mud at the water's edge, relishing the muddy sweet smell of damp earth and the breeze.

Reluctantly leaving the valley behind, and Eden a dream, we wound our way through a gentle pass through the hills around the valley. It was hot again but the changing landscape from desert, to field, to little settlements was a welcome distraction from the temperature and the distance.

Most of the buildings in the little mud villages we passed through had shuttered windows and doors made of metal, usually padlocked shut. Were they inhabited and if so, where were the people who lived in them? I never did find out.

---

[6] Kathleen Raine, Collected Poems, Faber and Faber Ltd, 2000

Occasionally we would see groups of young children, who despite the heat were often wearing woolly jumpers. The girls would have bright coloured head scarves and plainer skirts, often with thick woollen stockings underneath; the boys were more westernised, with jogging bottoms or jeans. The Berbers here were slim and fine-featured, often with beautiful bronzed skin and dark eyes.

They would smile at us shyly and not rush to us with their hands outstretched, as they might in more tourist-frequented spots, and Moha would talk to them genially or try to make them laugh before slipping them a few little coins.

But then amongst the dead-eyed buildings we found an open door which led to a tiny shop, the only light inside coming from the opening. At first it only seemed to sell four ingredients: cans of oil, large bottles of water, some tins of sardines and bags of what looked like flour.

In a corner glowed a fridge, and in it were a few bottles of grenadine and a milk drink. Cold! We bought the entire stock, and afterwards we sat like mischievous schoolboys in the muddy rutted street, Moha drinking four bottles and I three.

Our search for cold liquid became a little obsessive and later that day we found an even bigger place and bought a couple of bottles of chilled pulp of apple and orange plus some plastic cups. Once again, sitting against a wall, we toasted ourselves and waited for the mules, Hassan and Muhammad to catch us up.

I think between us, Moha and I were by then developing a real sense of achievement. We knew we had come a long way and, if we could keep up this pace, we would make it. Looking back, I think that we felt Eden had offered us some sort of benediction over our travels and that, whatever the trials before and ahead, we would muddle on through. A notion that would matter when we reached the last stage of our journey.

Sometime later Muhammad and Hassan arrived. We were into the last few days with our travelling companions, for we would leave them in Zagora where we would have to swap the mules for camels, the mules not being suitable for the desert sands we would then be facing.

I sensed that an end of expedition fizziness was running through them, which added to our own feelings of wellbeing, and the joking and teasing that had been lost in the Anti-Atlas and with the disappearance of Black was seeping back.

Eventually that day we found ourselves at the edge of a tiny town and we set up camp on the dirt football pitch. In the usual way, Moha and I dumped sleeping mats on the ground. I soon drifted off to sleep.

Later I awoke to see an old, battered Mercedes-Benz had pulled up. A smart -looking young policeman wearing a dark uniform with a white belt and white holster holding his gun got out and walked over to me.

"Parlez-vous français?" he grinned.

"Un petit peu," I said, staggering up and shaking his hand. Somehow it feels very vulnerable to be lying on your back being questioned by an armed man.

"Parlez-vous anglais?"

"Un petit peu aussi," he said smilingly and then, "You like it here in Morocco?"

"Certainement, I love it," I said. I assumed he wasn't being ironical about me sleeping on a football pitch.

"Then it is yours!" he said, waving his arms to expansively to include an amazing sunset.

And then he said something to Maha, who by now had joined us.

"He says I have to look after you very well," Maha translated.

The policeman, with another grin, went to inspect the contents of the bags that the mules were carrying. Not the personal bags, but the sacks of oats, boxes of flour and other provisions. Mohammed handed him a glass of mint tea, which he genially drank whilst inspecting the oats.

Apparently satisfied, he came back, wished me a great visit and drove off.

I was just making my sarcophagus arrangements for another night of sleeping outside when another official on a rickety old moped and wearing a football hoodie rode up and asked for all our passports, or identity cards, and a piece of paper to write all the details down. Moha looked apoplectic but I took the signal not to argue.

Later that night, another policeman turned up, shone his torch in our eyes and drove off. This bureaucratic oversight was starting to get out of hand.

But then I thought to myself, "Okay, what I am doing is odd. Even extreme perhaps? Moha is having to explain this mad Englishman to every petty official we come across."

I thought this as I lay with the wisps of night cloud coasting over the half familiar constellations. Back home, we would probably arrest, disturb or generally bother anyone choosing to sleep on a football pitch, so why should I expect otherwise out here? After all, I had discovered Eden.

Chapter 11: There May Be Dwarfs

The next morning, we set off early. The previous day had been a good one, I reflected. We had covered plenty of miles and I was coping well. Moha was full of his genial self-composure and the boys and the mules were plodding on placidly. We climbed up and away from our overnight camp, stopping to rest mid-morning on a high escarpment overlooking a blasted valley. As Moha smoked one of his powerful cigarettes, I sipped on some water and gazed upon the broad landscape of the Draa valley.

"I don't suppose we'll see any dwarfs here?" I said out loud, remembering one of the peculiar objectives of my expedition.

And then perhaps a little sadly I said: "No dwarfs anywhere."

Moha looked at me quizzically.

"Do you really know what dwarfs are?" I asked.

We had talked about them several times. It was not an English word he knew. I had tried the French *nain,* and he had rather unconvincingly nodded his head when I had asked him if he understood.

Moha then delivered a bombshell.

"Oh yes," he said in a kind of shrug-your-shoulders-of-course-what-a-silly-question kind of way. "Little people, they live in the village near Imlil, very short. They help with the mules."

I looked at him with surprise.

"Where?" I asked

"M'zik," he replied, which turned out to be a village a couple of miles from where we started whose name means 'small'.

I looked at Moha. The suspicion that he was teasing me was replaced by the thought that cultural misunderstanding is a subtle and elusive phenomenon. What if Moha's confusion when we started about searching for dwarfs was not because we were looking for the right translation but because it was a stupid question? What if dwarfs were in plain sight, so self-evident that looking for them was bizarre?

Later, back in England I came across someone other than the earnest Robert Grant Halliburton who also believed there to be dwarfs in these mountains.

Walter Harris is one of those larger-than-life characters from another age. He was for several decades a special correspondent for the *Times* in Morocco and lived there. A master of languages including French, Spanish and Moroccan Arabic, with his dark skin and fine features, in disguise he could pose successfully as a native Moroccan. As such he travelled into the heart of old Morocco and the mountains, places inaccessible to most Europeans. Living in Tangiers and of independent means, he took pleasure in social climbing and involving himself as a confidant of three different sultans, assorted viziers, tribal chiefs including the Glaoui brothers, and various brigands especially the mountain chieftain Raisuli. This last relationship was born out of Harris being kidnapped by the brigand and threatened in a jovial but meaningful way, with a protracted and painful death, if the ransom demands were not met.

His book on Morocco, published in the 1920s and called *Morocco That Was* is a wonderfully engaging account of his life there. He comes down through history as one of those eccentric, debonair, supremely confident individuals with an imperturbable air of *sang froid* and *savoir faire*, a lesser Lawrence of Arabia. If they made a movie of his life, he would have been played by George Clooney or Ryan Gosling. As a character, he appeared in an episode of *The Young Indiana Jones Chronicles*.

Although his book makes no mention of dwarfs, I found in the collected papers of Robert Grant Halliburton a letter Harris had written to the *Times* indicating his support for Halliburton and detailing several encounters he had with these people.

In his correspondence, he details visiting a place called Amzmiz, which lies at the foot of the west side of the Atlas Mountains not too far from Imlil, from where I had started my journey. Here he met a soldier who, the governor had told him, was a dwarf from this region. Harris describes him as 'slightly over four feet, certainly under four feet six, of reddish-brown colour, with a smooth face except for a few hairs on the chin, and dressed in the ordinary costume of a government cavalry soldier.'

Later he travelled through the province of Masuda and Mjat near the bashalik of Dueran. Here he was 'brought face-to-face with members of these small tribes, leading caravans of donkeys driven by seven men, none of whom was certainly above four feet six in height. They were of various ages, one almost a boy, the others older. One wore a thick grey beard and one a small black beard. They seemed more surprised and amused to see us than we to see them.'

Harris goes on to ponder whether these were indeed a 'race' of dwarfs or just a tribe of people living fiercely independent lives up in the high Atlas Mountains whose hard life had stunted their growth. Whatever their origins, they shared the fiercely independent spirit of the Berber people and more. The Governor of Amzmiz had complained to Harris that although they were nominally under his jurisdiction, they did not acknowledge the authority of the government or feel compelled to pay any taxes.

Harris describes them as a 'wild people, living in houses built in the rocks and snow, hunting mouflon with extraordinary agility and given to shooting anyone penetrating into their domains'.

Like Moha, he wondered if the fact that they were not spoken of by others is that 'their neighbours consider them as nothing extraordinary, and more particularly because, being independent, they are unable to descend the northern slopes of the Atlas to buy grain as they are imprisoned by their nominal governors wherever they are caught'.

Was it a coincidence that Harris found the dwarfs looking after donkeys, a role which Moha had told me they still fulfilled today?

Moha's comments made me think that perhaps I should take more seriously my search for evidence of dwarfs, which I had begun playfully and fancifully. The challenge was where and

– as I could see now - *how* to look. Where to start remained a problem.

Although I had Haliburton's account, it was not easy to find all the places named in his letter. This is perhaps not surprising, for all these names are approximations in English or French of local names in different dialects.

The Basahlik of Dueran mentioned by Harris is one such mystery. I could find neither a reference to a Bashalik or a place called Dueran. I did find the word Pashalik, which is an area governed by a Pasha, so perhaps that was what it was. And perhaps Dueran was not a place but was the name of some forgotten minor potentate.

In all the old books and reprints I have found about Morocco there is always this challenge. The names and places in them do not easily sit upon a modern map.

It is easy to believe that in a world satellite-mapped to the precise millimetre that the days of exploration have ended. In truth they have hardly begun. Place, and memory and story are combined in a way that is mysterious and confusing. All this brought it home to me that many paths lie through the same landscape and this is precisely their compelling attraction. Perhaps, I thought, exploration was less about seeking and more about being mindful. My vision of getting to the dunes of the Sahara compelled a certain path with little time to search for possibly fictitious places not along the way. If dwarfs were out there, then I should be ready to see them.

We plodded on thoughtfully and stopped for lunch in the shade of palm and tamarind trees. Shortly before stopping there was a rather curious moment when a very striking looking woman crossed our path as we walked through a deserted tiny village. She was probably in her late 20s or early 30s, elegantly dressed in a blue djellaba trimmed and patterned with gold. She was most unusually very forward in engaging in conversation, particularly with Moha. The conversation ended and we moved on. He looked embarrassed and was evasive when I asked him what the conversation was about. Her name, he said, was Sophia but who she was and what her circumstances were I could not find out.

Not for the first time, and particularly thinking about our conversations about dwarfs I thought of how difficult it was to see what was really there even when it was right in front of you. And if understanding one other person was so difficult then understanding a whole people was really impossible. Maybe it's the Berber people themselves that particularly confound our 'knowing'; but I suspect not. As a Westerner, no, given this train of thought, a *British* westerner, I cannot say I really understand, although I have met and stayed with them, the bushmen of Southwest Africa, the Hong Kong Chinese, even the French! I can read that the Berber people are followers of Islam and know that they are. But I also sense that another older set of beliefs entwine themselves around the spirit of this people. If questioned, Berbers are very elusive and guarded in their responses, yet subtle reminders of this other world can be seen. In the mountains, the refuges of living saints can be found and being a saint can be a family business stretching over generations. The relationship of these saints with rest of the population was arcane and shamanistic, particularly with the women of the High Atlas Mountains.

We should not find peculiar this idea of a more ancient belief system hiding in the shadows of a formal and 'approved' one. In France as late as the start of the 20th century, in remote regions, the local churches would hold Mary as their primary object of devotion, echoing the prehistoric worship of the Earth Mother as the source of fertility and renewal. Second in their devotion was Joseph, with Jesus himself coming a distant third. The local Catholic priest would find it expedient and wise not to challenge this too much.

As the day wore on, we walked for miles through a narrowish gorge. After a while it opened out to a flattish area on which a group of boys had placed goalposts marked by old shirts and were playing a ferocious game of football in bare feet. We sat on an old rock whilst Moha smoked another of his French cigarettes, and I sipped reluctantly on some warm water from my bottle.

"A sight from anywhere in the whole wide world!" I said to Moha.

He nodded his head and then called out to some of the boys something in Berber. One of them seemed to respond by launching a vicious and upending tackle on another.

"What did you say?" I asked.

"I told them you were a famous football manager from Chelsea!"

The game now continued at a more ferocious pace. A couple of minutes later I witnessed an amazing piece of dribbling wizardry in which one barefoot lad passed the desperate lunges of almost the entire opposition, ignored an open goal and dribbled back to his own goal line. He then repeated the entire run to show it wasn't a fluke and curled a low drive through the legs of a static and awestruck keeper. The young man looked at me, hands on his hips and head to one side as if to say:

"Come on, sign me then!"

I gave him a thumbs up and asked Moha to tell him to practise shooting with both feet if he wanted to make it to the top, and we headed on.

We camped on a ledge of land above an old dirt track which ran from the last village we had come through; it was late twilight when we stopped and set up. I arranged my bedding so my feet were towards the ledge; it was only a drop of a couple of metres on the other side, but I didn't fancy rolling over in my sleep and falling onto to the earth and rock below. The night gathered around me and I lay down, put my head on my backpack and stared at the stars. Hassan and Muhammad were chattering softly together, the single gas burner hissed into life, and one of the mules shuffled in the dark, sentry-like. Moha sat a little way away, listening to a group of young men chanting somewhere in the darkness. Weirdly beautiful, a mule stood huge and silhouetted against an enormous moon which was eye level to the horizon.

Maybe it was the long days on the road, maybe the sense of fatigue but I was struck again by a feeling of having slipped through to another world. It was not just that home felt far away but now completely somewhere else. I felt that where I was had in some ways a different dimensionality of place and time. Maybe the notion of dwarfs invisible in plain sight had loosened my sense of certainty such that even the familiar seemed to be casting an unfamiliar shadow.

If Marrakech still carries the footprint of the French and thereby the European – two mountain ranges and deserts separated me from the history and culture of my roots – here I was truly in another world and one which, I was increasingly aware, I did not much understand.

Which was the point at which a large dark head appeared at my feet above the ledge, babbling furiously, with wild white eyes rolling and staring at me. In the darkness the head appeared disembodied, as if floating in the air. A head that was agitated and upset and trying to tell me something. Something I could not understand but was clearly very important. There was desperation, fear and frustration all rolled into one and a dark desire.

I leaned up on my elbows, my legs refusing to respond and my brain racing to decide what to say or do.

At this point Moha emerged from the tent followed by a scowling Muhammad. They stood looking authoritatively down on the head, which raised itself a little to reveal it also owned shoulders. Moha's stare and voice as he spoke were stern and the head looked submissive.

Moha gave him some small coins and most importantly a couple of cigarettes. At which point the head and the shoulders, still babbling but now smiling, disappeared into the darkness.

Moha shrugged his shoulders and asked me if I was okay.

"Certainly," I said.

To Moha's increasing exasperation, the head returned twice more that night. To me, lost now in another world, it seemed hardly a surprise.

Chapter 12: Spies and Gorillas

The next day we were back on trail and back into the Eden-like world that was the long flat banks of the River Draa.

Back into the glades, into the pocket fields, the filtering sun. Three women dressed in the brightest of blue, burgundy and gold kaftans with beautiful African Berber faces, knelt at the edge of a little field cutting wheat with tiny scythes. Along the path, under the canopy, boys urged on donkeys laden with the harvest. In the river, two men with ancient heart-shaped shovels dug up the silt to make mud blocks for walls and houses. The sound was low and murmurous as frogs gurgled, birds lazily sang and the gentle sense of work being done was punctuated by the unexpected calls of the drovers. All was calm under the beneficence of the palms and the spell of the river.

As I walked, I tried to capture my thoughts about the way this landscape would impact upon me. It was, I thought, 'resonant'. That strange way that certain places can evoke an unconscious, not quite moment of recognition, but an elusive sense of connection perhaps, as if all around were somehow summoning something deep inside.

It is more captivating, more powerful than just an aesthetic appreciation of beauty or grandeur. It's a kind of alchemy which conjures a sense of returning to a place you've never been. It is as if an essential part of you has been recognised by an ineffable other.

The Portuguese have a word, *saudade*; it's like the Welsh word *hiraeth* (and the Cornish *hireth*). There is no easy

English translation. It's a kind of longing for a homeland that is in large part mythical.

But even this explanation doesn't quite do it. I remember my wonderful and ebullient friend David Brech, who had lived a large part of his life in Brazil and spoke fluent Portuguese, telling me that *saudade* recognised a natural world in which everything was alive and had spirit - even the very earth, the rocks upon it and all that is above.

But it was not just the fecund abundance around me that day which summoned such feelings. Dawns in the desert, sunsets in snow and ice and the whisper of the forest at night have also conjured such an emotion as haunted me at that moment.

We passed through the little village of Akelhouf and out along the river, at one point stopping to rest under the trees that grew on the riverbank. I knelt by the flowing waters, scooping the Draa river into my hands and letting it wash down my face. I felt as if I was kneeling in reverence and prayer in an act of homage to the moment. At that moment I looked up and saw a beautiful eagle circling above me, dipping its wings as it turned. I still do not know what sort of eagle it was. It had a light head and belly but its wings darkened towards their edges and finished in long, shadowy, feathered fingers. It may have been a Spanish Imperial Eagle, an occasional visitor to Morocco. It certainly was awesome in the deepest sense of the word.

The air seemed reluctant to move and we passed through several villages that seemed untroubled as yet by the internal combustion engine. As the sun rose higher, the landscape became more and more deserted. Again and again I noticed the principle by which old buildings, even quite grand ones, were left to decay and new ones built alongside to replace them.

But by now as well there was a real sense of walking towards the heart of Africa: people's faces were changing; in the villages the architecture hinted of differences originating from places beyond the mountains. Changes began to appear in the agriculture, moving away from the subsistence economy of locally grown products for local consumption to commercial growing, particularly of watermelons.

We stopped for lunch at such a farm where the owner had built a place of shade. Several mud-brick pillars supported long and wide branches to make a roof completed by a covering of long bamboo-like grasses. The local farmer wandered by and shook our hands, and returned with some cushions and fly swats made with split bamboo. He came back again a while later with a small round table upon which was a tray of cantaloupe and water melon pieces, cold as the first day of spring, sweet without being sugary and releasing a refreshing juice that trickled down your fingers as you ate.

Sometime that afternoon we crossed a metalled road two or three times as we maintained a direct route and the road itself curved and zigzagged around the contours of the land. Apart from the very occasional old truck laden to the skies with watermelons there was nothing on the road except...

"We are being followed," said Moha.

"Who or what by?" I asked.

"Wait till we cross the road again, you'll see."

A kilometre or two further on we came across the road again. It was completely empty.

"What's this all about?" I asked.

"Ssshh!" replied Moha. And he signalled me to move a little way off the road.

We listened, and for a while all I could hear was the incidental sounds of a not-quite silent landscape. Then in the distance – faintly at first – the put-put-put of an ancient sit-up-and-beg, two-stroke motorcycle. Through the heat haze an old man in a white djellaba wearing a peaked white crash helmet came into view, staring straight ahead. Just as he passed us Moha stood up suddenly and waved at him. The motorbike swerved and snaked for a few seconds before continuing towards the shimmering horizon.

Moha grinned and told me he had thought we were being followed for the last couple of days. When I asked him why he just shrugged his shoulders. Whatever the reason, the mystery continued for another couple of days. If we ever crossed the road, wherever we were, you could guarantee that one of three old men would drive past, turning a little way up the road, and then potter back the way they came, trying not to look at us as we waved. I began to understand that my expedition was now of 'official concern'. This old man was a member of some sort of internal security organisation. To this day I don't know whether I was under surveillance or protection.

That night we camped under some palm trees in a field that was lying fallow, a little way from two or three farmhouses. We were starting to be a bit short of food so it looked like it was to be a vegetable tagine again, except that we really didn't have any water.

However, the innate hospitality of Berbers once again kicked in. Without asking, someone wandered by and left a flagon of cool well water and a tin cup. Someone else dropped by with some watermelon.

After that, three young boys turned up with a loaf of bread and shook hands with each of us. I gave them five dirhams each for the courtesy, but they were equally delighted with the squares of soft cheese they were given and the glass of mint tea. What got them most excited was when they noticed the notebook I was writing in. I wished I had one to give each of them, so entranced were they. Moha and Hassan chatted away to them in Berber and I went back to writing up my notes. If I looked up as I wrote I would see three faces almost touching mine, peering at the book. I let them flick through the pages which they did with incredulous fascination. I asked them to sign their names which they did, laughing and pushing each other.

The next day, packing up camp with my usual ritual of careful personal hygiene and stowing of key items such as water bottles, we set off for the last hike of this section, all the way to Zagora. Moha as usual was calling it a short and easy walk. I didn't fall for that! Which was just as well, as by mid-afternoon, having started at 8.00 that morning, it was 38° and we were having to stop to cool down. My feet were very sore and blistered and two more sessions as guests of the police had taken its toll on my *joie de vivre*. The first of them of them was tea with the local police chief and the other was at a check point on the way into Zagora, where I sat in the blazing sun trying to look uncontroversial while Moha endeavoured to explain to some very suspicious officers what we were trying to do. Their looks of incredulity and disbelief reached across the language divide.

However all proved well and with backslaps, handshakes and a kiss or two we set off again, getting to the Little Kasbah, a place on the other side of town. Here, gratefully and wearily, I took off my filthy disgusting clothes, put on some shorts and lay in the small rectangular pool onto which the six rooms of the Kasbah opened. It was a lovely spot. The pool was small - three vigorous strokes would take you from one end of it to the other – but it was cool and clean. Around it three argan trees grew and up the walls of one side of the pool grew pink and yellow Bougainvillea and Jasmine.

After sleeping for a couple of hours, I drank fresh orange juice after fresh orange juice; it had become my drug of choice in the heat.

Mohammad and Hassan would be returning to their village early the next morning with their ever-patient mules loaded onto a pick-up, so that evening we all ate together on the roof of the Kasbah.

It was a moving moment; despite the differences of language and culture we had become a team. The four us had photographs taken together and we look proud. There was a sense of achievement, a feeling that we had collectively done something. Something perhaps rare, perhaps even unique. Certainly, we had seen no other hikers apart from the

Canadian heading west that we had bumped into in Ouzazarte.

I imagined all the conversations that Moha had had so far: with the Imman, the school children in the villages, the farmers, the donkey men who had stopped us on our way. And of course, conversations along the following lines with the various brigades and bodies of Moroccan policing.

"Where are you going?"

"To M'hamid."

"Where have you come from?"

"From Telouet."

"Walking all the way?"

"Yes."

"Wow! Why?"

"I am looking after him!" Pointing at me.

"Who is he?"

"An Englishman."

"Ah, why is he doing it?"

"I guess he likes walking ..."

Looking back, I think I was starting to feel like Forrest Gump.

Or a large circus animal.

A few nights previously, whilst sleeping in a watermelon patch, three policemen in different uniforms, plus the village busybody, turned up. I struggled to my feet (see note earlier about not lying down when talking to people armed with revolvers), but Moha gestured for me to sit down, so I sat on the floor whilst they discussed things overhead.

"Do you know how to look after him?"

"What do you feed him on?"

"Can we see your gorilla permit?"

"You should be very careful, bringing a gorilla into this region."

So it was with the sense that these two guys had committed themselves to an adventure which would never have made more than passing sense to them that I said goodbye. Sure, they were paid for the journey and I gave them, as is customary, a large tip for their trouble; but nevertheless it was with a real sense of a band of brothers that we chinked our glasses of mint tea and bade each other adieu.

However, that was not to be our final goodbye. Their plan was to set off very early the next morning with the mules tethered together on a flatbed pick-up, but when Moha and I set out after mid-morning for a walk around Zagora, they were still there. One mule was standing placidly on the flat bed, the other was standing on the ramp before it, unmoving and immovable. If the world needed a statue to the power of passive aggression that mule would have been it. Muhammad, sweating with exertion, was pulling on a rope tied to the mule's head; Hassan and assorted others were pushing at the rear end; and nothing much was happening. Personally, I could sympathise with the idea of standing up for a few hours on the back of a truck as it circled around the mountains. Hassan and Muhammad stopped to politely say goodbye again and Moha and I headed into town.

When we got back about two hours later all was as before, only now with a much bigger crowd of advisers. One mule stood peaceably on the truck and the other still immovably at the start of the ramp. Moha and I diplomatically crept in to the Kasbah through a side door, sensing much pride was at stake for all concerned. Moha told me later that the reluctant mule had eventually capitulated after another two hours.

Chapter 13: Don Quixote and Sancho Panza

Two days later I was hunkered down in an old desert tent made of round steel poles and a thick, woollen cover. We were in a rocky, gritty wilderness, featureless and seemingly infinite. I was lying on an old, tattered bed mat. Not far from me, Moha snored and coughed in his cigarette-filled sleep. Over in the corner near the entrance, Zain, the camel captain, sat in meditative silence, eyes half closed. It was 40° at least and a hot wind blew steadily, rocking the sides of the tent. Every so often a spiteful gust would lift the side and it was as if one of those industrial space heaters had suddenly been turned on, blasting superheated air across us all.

It was between midday and the first hour of the afternoon. We had no intention of moving until after 4.00 pm so the only thing to do was lie still, conserve water and listen to the wind. Outside the camels had been unloaded of their packs and hobbled so they could not stray – a strategy which the following few days would prove not to be that effective.

Zain, who had joined us with his three camels as we set of from Zagora, was a true desert man, with a dark weather-beaten skin on a face chiselled and fine. He had brown intelligent eyes and his head was permanently wrapped in a *tagelmust*[7], the long headscarf wrapped like a turban to provide insulation against the heat. It would also be used to cover up his face against the dust and sand whipped up by the wind. Like the Bedouin I had met in the Egyptian Sahara,

---

[7] Also known as a *shemagh*.

he went about the commonplace tasks of desert crossing and survival with a graceful economy of movement and real skill.

Earlier that day, Moha and I had crested a ridge to see him single-handedly putting up the tent, which was large and very heavy, by pointing the one end of the tent into the wind to let the gusts inflate it and take its weight whilst he erected the supporting poles and pinned down the sides. It was up and ready with the camels hobbled before we had caught up with him.

I was starting to realise that we would need all his desert skills. Back in Zagora, after Muhammad and Hassan had left, Moha and I had sat in the bustling main street having a short bitter coffee and making plans.

"This is going to be hard, Steve," he said.

"It is very hot now and we won't be able to move during the middle of the day. The problem is do we go slower and take longer, but then we might run out of water, or do we keep going and find it too tough?"

I said I couldn't really decide. He knew how fit I (or not) I was. It was his call, I told him. Which in retrospect was simultaneously the right decision and a selfish one.

"OK," he said thoughtfully, "we will aim to do it in four or five days."

Which in my rough calculations would be more than eight hours of walking a day in temperatures over 400.

"It's not all desert," said Moha, thoughtfully. "Just most of it."

So we had met Zain and his three camels on the outskirts of Zagora to set off on the final third of the journey. I was feeling footsore and travel weary by now but also determined. Five days in my head felt like a manageable amount. It was less than I had done to date after all.

I had also gone to an old market in town and bought some fruit powders to add to the warm water we were going to carry in big old plastic water carriers. After my experience in the desert on the other side of the Anti-Atlas mountains and the mountains themselves I was determined to find a way to keep better hydrated. The problem was that I just couldn't swallow the water that became hotter and hotter during the day. I reckoned that making up a fruity drink might be more palatable and also give me the advantage of taking on board some sugars as I trekked. I also planned to make the drinks in the middle of the night when the water got really cold and then insulate them by wrapping cloth around them and keeping them in the camels' panniers out of the sun during the day. In fact, Zain soon showed me a good trick whereby you soak the cloth – thick, hairy Berber wool was best – and then hang it from the camels' saddlebags as they moved along. Almost miraculously, the evaporation effect of doing this meant that the drink inside stayed cool all day.

The going had been good so far despite the intense heat. We had left the main road at Amezrou and headed down the old camel routes along the Draa valley winding through the villages along the way.

Earlier in the morning, as we sheltered in the meagre shade of a hollow under a solitary small acacia tree, I said suddenly to Moha:

"You know, I think this is crazy!"

He looked at me questioningly, then replied,

"Absolutely, very crazy!"

We both laughed and I told him about Don Quixote and his quest.

"Who is he?" I was asked.

"An old man who wanted to take on the world as a Knight, and who was saved from killing himself several times by his trusty good friend Sancho Panza." I paused a second.

"That would be you, Moha my friend!"

"It's been a pleasure Steve... but it is crazy!"

Cervantes perhaps had it right:

When life itself seems lunatic, who knows where madness lies? Perhaps to be too practical is madness. To surrender dreams — this may be madness. Too much sanity may be madness — and maddest of all: to see life as it is, and not as it should be!

Although I think I was never more than half a day's long walk from some sort of settlement it was easy to imagine the camel trains heading from Timbuktu towards the oases in the Draa Valley. It was a fraught and dangerous journey. The weather, the terrain, the emptiness, the danger of attack would have conspired to make the journey's end doubtful and a massive relief.

James Gray Jackson described it thus in 1811[8]:

These akkabahs (several camel trains moving together) consist of several hundred loaded camels... During their route they are often exposed to attacks of roaming Arabs of Sahara, who generally commit their depredations as they approach the confines of the desert.

In this fatiguing journey, the akkabahs do not proceed in a direct line across the trackless desert to the place of their destination, but turn occasionally eastward or westward, according to the situation of certain fertile, inhabited, and cultivated spots, interspersed in various parts of the Sahara, like islands in the ocean called oases; these serve as watering places to the men, as well as to feed, refresh and replenish the hardy and patient camel: at each of these oases, the akkabahs adjourn about seven days, and then proceeds on its journey, until it reaches another spot of the same description. In the intermediate journeys, the hot and impetuous wind called a Schume, converts the desert into a movable sea... A sea without water, more dangerous than the perfidious waves of the ocean. In the midst of the latter the pilot always entertain some hopes but in these parching

---

[8] *An Account of the Empire of Morocco and The District of Suse.* Original printed in London 1811. My edition Forgotten Books, 2018.

deserts, the traveller never expects safety or cessation of the wind. If it continues, the most numerous caravans are often buried under mountains of sand... In 1805, a caravan proceeding from Timbuktu to Tafifelt was disappointed in not finding water at one of the usual watering places when, horrible to relate, the whole of the persons belonging to it, 2000 in number, besides 1800 camels perished thus of thirst.

And even if the wind didn't blow, there were other dangers. Friedrich Gerhard Rohlfs, on his travels, woke up to find his guide had just shot him and then swung a blade at his hand nearly severing it. In the end he was left for dead with nine wounds. Somehow he managed to survive for two days before being rescued by some passing tribesmen.

Sensing the apex of the heat had passed, Moha and Zain stirred and started to move. We found the camels, despite being hobbled, had wandered out of sight and over the horizon. Zain took nearly 40 minutes to find them, reappearing like a dot on the distance like Omar Sharif in the film *Lawrence of Arabia*.

As we set off again my intention had been to ride one of the camels for a while, to give my feet more time to recover, but less than twenty minutes of being jolted painfully around was more than enough and I dismounted.

It is a wonder that camels have passed muster as beasts of burden for millennia. There is no trick, it seems, to gain a comfortable mastery in riding them. The sensation is like a broken spoke motion: round, round, round, jolt!

Side saddle riding is not an affectation but a necessity. Sitting astride, as I had to, means that the nether regions of a male *Homo sapiens*, perched slightly up the hump, are always in imminent danger of sliding down at some speed into the metal bracket that sits on the front of the saddle.

Footsore I might have been, but walking produced less tears ...

But having said this, I had grown to love camels. I loved the way they gingerly put their feet down each time as if they had learned to never trust the ground beneath them. The way they formed their lips into an "O" when they are looking at you. Their languid curiosity when sticking their noses into each other's baskets. The way their eyes widened with faux delight when you offered them an old orange with the peel on it or an ancient courgette. I could not help thinking that at times they look ever so slightly sarcastic.

But the whole cultural history of the relationship between camels and their owners is intimate, perhaps a little odd and ancient. If the female camel loses a calf they can become very distressed and mourn for fully ten days. The Bedouin herdsman often make a stuffed camel calf toy for the female camel to keep as she grieves.

It may be the case, according to Robert Lewin in his book *Camel*[9], that male camels have a rudimentary knowledge of the stars and can navigate to an extent by them.

Camels have sex sitting down.

----

[9] Reaktion Books, 2020

I may also have the right to be wary of the advances of a camel in the night. The legendary desert explorer Wilfried Thesiger once said: "I can remember another camel that was attached to her Master as a dog might have been. At intervals throughout the night she came over, moaning softly, to sniff at him where he lay, before going back to graze."

We stopped one day and rested where we had found a little shade from some bushes. As the day cooled we started to get ready to move on. One of the camels, still hobbled, was kneeling down as Zain was loading heavy boxes into the panniers on its back in order that we might restart our journey. The boxes were behind him, and Zain would pick one up, turn and place it in the pannier. The camel was looking around with curiosity. Some little distance away it saw the juicy remains of a watermelon and started to crawl quite quickly towards it. Zain, with his back to the camel, failed to see this and turning around with some heavy tent poles found the near-to panniers had disappeared, over balanced and fell flat on his face.

We slept deeply and contentedly that night under a dozen huge palm trees until dawn when I groggily came round to be handed a jar of Nescafé, the kettle containing fairly warm water, some powdered milk and a glass.

I looked around. It was a beautiful spot, full trees bending over and nothing to the horizon of the volcanic rim that runs around the outside of the Draa Valley and in between the miles and miles of sand, grit and pebble desert punctuated by acacia trees. This lifted the spirits mightily. I think I was suffering a little with desert sickness, physically and emotionally tired of the heat, the monotonous and limited food and the endless feeling of just wanting to get there.

I watched Zain fixing a broken metal bracket on one of the frames which supported the large panniers on the camel's backs, using blue plastic twine until it had a kind of bandaged look about it, like a scrawny broken leg, but it proved effective. I suspected this temporary fixing would not be particularly 'temporary'. If it works, it will remain. Time and again I have noticed the Berber characteristic of 'if it is serviceable, use it'. The cardboard box that the jars and tins we used were kept in was torn and broken, and each stop entailed carefully undoing the miles of string that held it together to be followed later by methodical retying. There had been several occasions when we could have obtained a new box but there was no motivation to do so.

To Berbers, circularity, the reuse of materials and the avoidance of unnecessary waste is no new-fangled, environmentally sound idea, but an ancient and sustainable way of life.

It was like all the places we had stayed when we had not been bivouacking. They had been clean but not unnecessarily clean. If something was broken but not functionally broken it was kept and used. If it was dented or chipped, then why not? All life is. There often was a comfortable charm about this and an honourable simplicity. Stuff had value because it worked.

The night before as we sat in the dark, Moha had produced an enormous watermelon to finish off our dinner. He was attempting to cut it with a knife with a three-inch-long blade. I handed him my beautiful bush craft knife, superbly weighted with a wooden and bone handle and a super sharp blade etched with an abstract pattern. I am rather proud of it: it feels ancient, north European, something a Saxon or a Viking would have appreciated.

Moha took it without commenting on its wonders, only grateful for the length of the blade as he skilfully cut enormous fruit chunks. Later I showed Zain, pointing out its features, thinking it might engage his inner Berber warrior, but he only nodded politely and went back to picking the watermelon seeds out of his teeth with his own knife and spitting them into the darkness.

The next day proceeded much as the one before, with four hours of walking followed by a search for some shade. Three hours of not moving, forty-five minutes finding the mischievous camels, were followed by another three to four hours of walking till dark, to find myself lying on some firm sand in the gap between the circling hills.

In the dark, Maha sat smoking and drinking some of Zain's foul-tasting mintless tea. A hot wind blew through the gap in the hills. Moha and Zain had followed my example and not erected tents; instead Zain had made a windbreak from the panniers, the bags of equipment and then settled down to cook some soup. Somewhere out in the gloom the three camels were munching on a big bag of dates. Apart from the lamp Zain was using on his head, the only light in the sky was from the stars peering through some wispy clouds, with the moon not yet risen.

I reckoned it would be two more days till I got there. Not that I had picture of what getting there was, beyond the fact my destination must be undeniably desert. Which was paradoxical because now I had been walking through desert for several days. It was just not the right sort of desert. I soon fell asleep to the sound of camels breathing rhythmically with an ancient moan that surely had lulled the centuries into slumber. They rested about fifty metres from my feet looking like small hillocks in the gloom.

I stirred an hour or two later and noticed that one of them was much closer, but I thought nothing of it until a while later I realised the camel was now at my feet. I gave the camel a gentle kick, as one might a partner who was invaded your side of the bed, but the camel didn't move. I thought about this. Now the camel was a big beast and the idea of it rolling on top of me seemed a dangerous reality. 'Squashed by a camel' would be an odd epitaph, so I moved my sleeping mat and settled a distance away. After falling back to sleep, I was awoken an hour or two later by the malodorous breath of the same camel snoring into my ear.

Chapter 14: The End of The Road

As we had stopped the previous night, I had seen a light in the far distance and heard, on the slightest desert breeze, the evening adham or call to prayer sung with reverence by a muezzin. It was, even for a non-believer, a summoning to something hypnotic and beautiful. Somewhere beyond the rest of the day there would be a settlement. But that could be many miles away. Sound travels far in the flat world of the desert. I had once slept in the desert in Egypt, hearing like a whisper in the night the sound of a long train from a line nearly 40km distant.

It took a little while to get going. All the camels had gathered some little distance away and I went and fetched them back one by one. Eventually, with the camels loaded we set off towards the source of the prayers the previous night,

Gradually the rocks and the boulders, the strips of soft sand, mud and grit and the tamarind bushes started to give way to a band of high palms, out of which appeared a tall, handsome black African dressed in a blue djellabah and turban. He was riding on a donkey and towing a cart with pneumatic tyres. We were back, back with people, amongst the cultivated fields that lay on either side of the road. Through the trees rose up a first building made of big reddish mud blocks, much cruder than the ones earlier in our journey. We walked under the palms along a dirt path enjoying the cool of the shade as a kind of benediction and the benign sense of a wilderness dissolved.

Everyone here seemed to ride a donkey. Back in Zagora it was motorbikes and mules and pick-ups. People stared at us curiously, the children particularly, from faces that were no longer so much the fine-eyed olive-skinned ones found up in the villages of the High Atlas. Instead, like driftwood washed up from the sea of the desert, all the physiognomy of the continent looked at the decrepit Englishman staggering along following a camel.

So, for a brief beautiful time, the desert faded away and we found ourselves walking through little villages which looked very much like the Mexican pueblos you see in old western movies. It didn't seem improbable that John Wayne or James Stewart might ride down the main street on hard-nosed ponies.

I soon came across the modern fortress of a rich man's house. It was a large, two-storey building with dusky pink walls and white trimmings surrounded by a high wall with cruel barbs set in it like metal talons. There was a big vaulted gate - don't you love the rich?

But most houses were poor and communal and totally without ostentation.

In one of the villages, Ouled Yousf, we found a perfect village well at which we stopped to drink and rest.

A perfect well is one in the middle of the village where people can meet and talk and pass on practical help and mysterious knowledge. A perfect well is dark and deep and the water is always chilled. And its darkness is haunted by the voices of those who have stood above and imagined that they were un-listened to.

No wonder we believe that wells are full of spirits and enchantment, for they give life to generations and in return receive wisdom, which they give back to those who would listen,

One of my favourite poets, Seamus Heaney, celebrates the oozy mud magic of a well in his poem *Personal Helicon* and the gifts it endows.

... I rhyme,
To see myself, to set the darkness echoing.[10]

A well is a special place and I remembered the one back in the Anti-Atlas Mountains where we had camped and where Black had stood guard.

We stopped for a while. Zain sat on his haunches smoking a cigarette and holding one of the camels in thoughtful reverie whilst Maha and I, grinning like kids, poured water over ourselves.

There is something about water. No wonder our ancestors worshipped it. Whether it be the Druids and their ponds concealing the leathery corpses sacrificed to its life force or the river gods of the whole world and the seas and the oceans and the rain. It is worshipped where it is plentiful and where it is scarce. It is worshipped because it gives life and can take it away. The desert reminds you water is precious and deeply resonant.

The troubled and complex Gavin Maxwell, whose book had haunted and shaped this journey, chose to live near water at

---

[10] *Personal Helicon*, Seamus Heaney, Internet Poetry Archive.

a place he called *Camusfearna* at Sandaig Bay on the west coast of Scotland. Here he searched in vain for sanctuary and resolution to a life he often found intolerable.

His location was perhaps a search for that same sense of healing in which we give a dying man a drink.

Back in the deserts again towards evening, watching the setting of the sun and the way the sky turned sandy grey, we walked towards a low line of trees silhouetted against the gathering twilight. The odd tall palm rose above the others, feathered and bulbous at the top like a strange, giant thistle. For the first time in a while, I felt I was walking towards a somewhere. In this case the end of the road.

There was a steady rhythm to our plod now and even though my feet were sore and my face grimy and heatblasted tight, the ground was flat and locomotion was easy. The landscape seemed expansive and my mood fell in tune with that. This was to travel well. Morocco is a generous place, I thought. Not just the people here but the land itself is open to the traveller.

On this last night as I lay one once more on the ground it struck me quite forcibly that apart from that one night outside Ouarzazate with the mysterious near arrest, we had every night on our travels stopped when we were ready to, in a place on our way and where we chose.

The more I thought about it, the more for a Brit this was strange. In fact, it was nearly unthinkable back home in England. Back home, 'wild camping', as it is known, is a seriously controversial area, a legal minefield; and certainly to camp in this way would very probably result in an altercation with a bristling somebody, emphasising their 'rights'.

It wasn't always like this. Back home, the ancient tradition from Saxon times was that land was something held in common and a shared resource for the people who lived upon it. There were rights once to hunt, to grow, to water, to collect wood and the most basic right of all – to wander. Over time and in plain sight, this has been undermined by continuing huge acts of theft by a bunch of chancers known as the aristocracy and their wannabe parvenus.

It started with the Norman conquest and the resulting 400 years of occupation by the Norman French, whose first act was to remove a quarter of England from the ownership of its people so they could chase deer around on horses. By Tudor times, this land grab proceeded apace as laws were written, manipulated and rewritten. This continued into the 16th and 17th century where on the backs of hundreds of thousands of slaves and the wealth thereby created, more and more land was sequestered and fenced in. More than a third of the population who had depended upon this common land were left destitute and near starvation. The response of those in power to this problem was simply to declare being a vagrant illegal on the bizarre basis that if you make something illegal you solve the problem.

Today half of England is owned by 1% of the population, 92% of our countryside and 97% of our rivers are privately owned and we are not welcomed upon them.

In his wonderful work *The Book of Trespass*, Nick Hayes points out that the Duke of Buccleuch owns 270,000 acres of the British Isles, which is more than twice the size of the cities of Birmingham, Derby, Nottingham and Leicester put together. He writes:

'The elegant final flourish of this land seizure, comes from the Bourton estate, which now sells firewood, once a common right, back to the commoners at £95 per cubic metre.'[11]

It was, I thought, too easy to see the Glaoui as some avaricious foreign 'other' rather than representing the kind of which we have more than enough.

Another example, I mused, of something being hidden in plain sight. It had taken me nearly three weeks to spot that I could walk more or less where I wanted and sleep wherever I felt tired and that the people I met welcomed me rather than chased me off 'their land'.

We camped that night back in the grit and rubble that is much of the Sahara Desert. So, this was the last night. For the last time I rolled out the old foam mattress with its torn and tatty damask cover. For the last time I built my sarcophagus of cases and boxes. For the last time I carefully completed my "one-wipe" wash and used a few of the remaining drops of antibacterial gel to clean my hands. There was a real sense of ritual about it now and the embracing feeling of being centred and whole that it created.

Again I stirred at dawn and appreciated the time to get things ready. I had filled my water bottles before sleeping to allow

---

[11] *The Book of Trespass: Crossing the Lines that Divide Us*, Nick Hays, 2020.

them to get cold. I now put them in their old wool wraps tied up again with string and soaked them.

By the time we started it was already extremely hot. I grimly set off, telling myself as I consciously put one foot in front of the other that each was one more step towards the last one. At first the going was a mix of undulating grit and sand and rocks, similar to the previous day.

For one more time, we were back in the realms of desolation. The ground was baked mud and patterned like the scales of a great fish. I passed the bones of a camel face scattered on the ground. There was no road, no vegetation, just stones and rocks and sun. Ahead of me ran a ridge running from one edge of the horizon to the other. It looked steep and there seemed to be no way up it. At first I thought we were going to have to climb up, reversing the climb down of that very first day. Unless I had been living my life under the misapprehension that camels couldn't climb, the detour around for the camels, I contemplated, would be a long one.

As we approached though, it became apparent that there was a steep path, that rose like a switchback up the side. We made our way slowly and painfully, pausing in the burning heat on each turn until we eventually crested the ridge by an old watchtower.

Beyond it stretched the flatness of the far horizon towards the Algerian border. A hazy road lay below that would stretch to M'hamid, where in a day or two a driver from Kasbah would pick us up and take us home. Behind me lay into the distance the long path I had come, stretching back to another hazy ridge we had walked over yesterday and beyond that, smothered in the heat, a sense only of great mountains.

We wound our way back down the other side, my faithful walking poles thumping on earth and clicking on rock, and after crossing the road we headed off in a more direct line to our destination,

We stopped a couple of times to rest in the hollows by acacia bushes trying to drink away the heat. Moha was rightly keen to keep going.

"Just one and a half hours," he would say each time, "and then we can have a shower at the camp."

But the going got harder and the heat more intense and I felt overwhelmed. By now we were walking on soft sand, and it was particularly hard going. I began to struggle again, feeling my throat constricting.

And then suddenly there they were, not huge, but real and undeniable. Sand dunes. Not just sand but dunes gracefully curved by the wind.

And I knew, as I had known all along, that this was my goal. I had made it! M'hamid was a place on a map. It was a place of which I knew nothing. It was a point of convenience because it gave a name to where the dunes started.

From the mountains to the desert, I had said. And here I was. My adventure was done.

I felt a little proud of myself. This was my achievement, small and insignificant though it was. The slightly overweight bloke with a dodgy knee had walked from the High Atlas Mountains to the desert. I stood looking at them in wonder.

Filthy beyond belief, covered in sweat and with my lips stuck together with mucus and sugar I managed to croak out a 'thank you' to Moha and shook his hand.

I staggered over to first dune and, in the four inches of shade offered by an acacia bush in the midday sun, marked the waypoint on my GPS.

It read: N29. 51.479 W005 38.506.

I tried to speak to Moha but I was done. I took off the long cotton blue scarf I had been wearing as protection from the dust and heat and soaked it, wrapping it around my head to cool off. I was stained blue on my ears and shoulders for weeks afterwards.

We all smiled at each other and enjoyed the silence. Each of us was measuring our own journey and trying to make sense of it. I have photo of it. It is a very special image.

After about twenty minutes I climbed onto a camel and, much more comfortable this time as I could brace my feet on the panniers, I rode through the dunes to M'hamid.

Chapter 15: Telouet

The road into town was bleak and desolate. The sky became a strange colour somewhere between flax and gunmetal and to the left and right of the road, a little in the distance, small twisters rose into the air dragging up the crumbs of the earth. As if summoned by some unseen magical force they would appear and move in directions that seemed random and uncertain and then suddenly disappear. I thought about the snake on the trail way back.

Reaching the outskirts of M'hamid, we stopped for the night with a friend of Moha's who had built a Berber campsite. It was collection of low, mudbrick buildings, a toilet block and communal kitchens. There were three or four rooms and large tents in the Berber style. Mud and grit paths separated the buildings and tents and shade was provided by medium-high palms. There were also a couple of Berber salons, large rooms around which ran a continuous cushioned bench upon which you could sit or sleep.

I chose one of the rooms, hoping the fan there would reduce some of the heat. That was a bad mistake. I think that probably was the hottest night I had spent so far. It just never really cooled off. The heat retained by the mud walls more than cancelled out the efforts of the enormous, ancient, clanking fan. I slept very little and was fully awake by six. Feeling I was trying to sleep in a slow cooker, I got up and wandered around the campsite. I planned to write some notes in my journal but the night had left my brain sluggish and confused.

Zaid found me sitting outside at a table under hexagonal bamboo shade and went and found some breakfast. Alongside the old trail food there was stale bread, processed cheese and, my latest innovation to avoid the tobacco tasting mintless mint tea, my dried milk and Nesquik chocolate combo. Somewhere Zain found an egg which we fried and shared.

This was not quite the scenario when had I set off the day before to walk the final section of my trek. I think I had been dreaming of aircon, white sheets, a swimming pool and a menu. But hey ho, I could see the intention was good and my disappointment reflected more my unreconstructed Western needs than anything else. And such needs would assuredly be met today as, after we had got here yesterday, we had found a hotel we could move into to wait for the truck that would take us back to Marrakesh.

M'hamid seemed a half-way to nowhere place: strange, remote, on the borders with Algeria and for many years a restricted area. Five decaying Kasbahs lay around it. For years it was a small, self-sustaining little oasis where nomads and caravans might stop to rest and replenish. But the inexorable creep of the desert, climate change and a fungus that attacks the paLm trees had left it struggling, sustained by the military and hardier tourists seeking to drive 4x4s wildly over the dunes.

My sense already was that here the potential for the incongruous lurked as it had already on so much of my journey.

This had proved to be the case on the previous evening with a hotel we had first stumbled upon. It was built in the traditional style of a wide arched door leading to a shaded courtyard from which a staircase climbed to the rooms on three levels above. It was quiet and empty and there was no one at the reception. No one seemed to be staying there. Then I noticed in a darkened corner a North African man sitting next to a Western woman with long dark hair. There were both looking at a laptop screen.

"Is there anyone working on reception?" I asked.

The girl with the long dark hair looked up.

"There doesn't seem to be," she said pleasantly but unhelpfully.

The accent was American, probably Californian.

"The owner should be back soon," she said more helpfully.

"Are you staying here?" I asked, hoping for some trip advisor feedback before committing to the purchase of two rooms.

"Sort of," she said, "we're kind of working here too."

"What kind of work?" I asked.

"I paint the hotel signs and he," indicating her friend, "he mends the shades."

For a hotel that didn't even run to a receptionist this did seem an over-specification of roles.

At that point the hotel owner returned. He turned out to be a car dealer from Amsterdam who had bought this hotel. He showed us round. The hotel was a little worse for the wear, but clean enough and unoccupied.

"You can choose any room," he said. "The water can be a bit unreliable but it is working at the moment."

But in the end, we did not stay there. There weren't many to choose from but I did find one that had a bar, a pool, the guarantee of running water and staff.

And now next morning I thought about the strange American girl and wondered what narrative had brought her to this little military town on the border with Algeria. Where had she come from? Where was she going to? In my life of travelling I have found that there is no place, howsoever remote or lost or unremarked, in which you will not run into a Californian girl passing through. I remembered my friend Peter Schwartz, a New Yorker who lived in California and thereby armed with the necessary sense of the absurd, telling me how on a student trawl round Europe he had found, in a youth hostel in the centre of Sicily, an entire community of West Coast refugees residing, some of whom had been in residence for a decade or more. He assumed that wealthy parents, exasperated by their idealistic buffoonery, paid them an allowance to remain but not enough to go home. And so, they lived on, gathering each evening together to eat the meal of the day provided, which was always Spaghetti Pomodoro with meatballs.

Later that morning Moha and I moved into the hotel we had found. And there I washed off the dirt and the grime but not the sense of strangeness of being off the trail. I felt in kind of limbo land, stuck somewhere between the wilderness and the modern world. Ready to leave, but like Peter's community, not ready to return.

We headed into M'hamid that evening and I found Moha in an equally reflective mood. We sat in a café at sunset, watching a scene as timeless as the desert itself as people wandered in groups and alone along the dirt street, the open shops filled with vegetables, washing powder, cloth, large cans of oil and one or two half-hearted vendors trying to sell T-shirts.

Moha suddenly said:

"You know, you are very brave and very tough. When people ask me about what we are doing they all say that."

I've never thought of myself as being brave, in fact often the opposite. Thinking about it now, being brave isn't a quality, it's an absence of other things – fear, imagination or perhaps in this case, for me, insight.

I had no conception of how hot it would be and the difference a start a month later than originally anticipated would make to things. I've never felt either that I had grasped fully that 570 km in three weeks might be a long way.

Couple that with an inability to recognise various physiological warning signs when my body is signalling enough is enough and you have a man stupid enough to walk into the desert in late May.

In the traditional meaning of brave, the bravest thing I probably did was, after I sat down dizzy and exhausted under that acacia tree, to accept and embrace the fact that I had met my goal, climb onto that camel and reject the imagined judgements of others.

As we drove back the next day in a Toyota 4x4, through the blasted rocks with the watchtowers, the rubble-strewn wilderness that I had been sweating through for days, so little time ago, seeing the winding path up to the escarpment in which I had made myself take 100 steps before I would stop to catch my breath and open my arms to catch to faintest cooling breeze, I realised that I loved Morocco more than any other place of the planet. We passed a man selling just four watermelons, sitting on the side for road. A car, a Mercedes I think it was, had stopped and a man in a pale blue djellabah was walking back to buy one. I smiled remembering how central watermelons had been to my existence just a day or two before.

It took us two days to drive to Marrakesh and we stopped at Zagora at the end of day one.

We stayed in the Kasbah Sirocco along with a motorcycle posse of big middle-aged jowly Dutchmen and Germans, who came in in black leathers with their equally well upholstered companions as we checked in.

Zagora comes to life in the evenings. I wanted to buy a Berber flag which I promised I would fly at my next gig. Walking along the streets, past the tin door of shops selling Michelin tyres, authentic Berber souvenirs, Toureg scarves, coffee shops, a sign saying *Alimentation Générale*, we bumped into the strange Californian girl and her boyfriend with the Rastafarian dreadlocks whom we had met back at the hotel.

Moha spotted them first. I was quite disconcerted. I had spent at least a couple of hours over the last few days making up a narrative about them. Instinctively I had known she was one of those people who do not follow the conventional rules of conversation.

They stopped, she gave an exaggerated bow, and I told her the where and the how of this adventure. I told her about my walk in search of the spirit of the Berbers and of dwarfs and warlords. She told me about going back to the US as her father had died. She clearly had ambivalent feelings about this, although her family were very excited, so that to avoid the fuss she was then going to go canoeing with her sister in the North Washington State. I told her to keep an eye out for the spirit bears that live there. She told me our meeting wasn't an accident and proposed that we connect by Facebook. But of course we never did.

That night I wrote down her imagined story as a ballad and later put it to music.

Moroccan Song

Words: Steve Bonham. Music: Steve Bonham and John Humphreys

It's a dirty, thirsty, cracked up street,
With a Coke sign over the bar,
Where a watermelon man, sells sunshine gold,
In the remains of the old bazaar.
And the gapped toothed fellow, and the cat with one eye
Keep a watch on things as they pass,
Under a Tamarind tree, by the old village well,
Drinking sweet mint tea from a glass

There's a California girl, who's been a long time on the run,
With an email from her mother, and a message from her
    brother
Saying we're so sorry that you've gone.
It's a dirty, thirsty, cracked up street,
With a Coke sign over the bar,
Where a watermelon man, sells sunshine gold,
In the remains of the old bazaar.

They've built world from wood and straw,
And mud from the river bed,
But the California girl, is more concerned,
About the things going on in her head
The genie in the bottle, that granted her three wishes
Then sailed her over the sea
To the Tamarind tree, by the old village well
And some sunburned geography.

Where the California girl, is painting hotel signs
She's something to confess, won't say her life's a mess
But nothing seems to fit or rhyme
They've built world from wood and straw,
And mud from the river bed,
But the California girl, is more concerned,
About the things going on in her head

The lights go out round the swimming pool
There's a twister over the dunes,
The California girl is out there walking
In the shadows of a dead-eyed moon
While the man who bought the hotel, and the boy who makes
     the shades
Have wrapped themselves in blue
Smoking old Moroccan, believing they're forgotten
From a bad time point of view.

They share a memory, like the rain in mid July
Of the world's perpetual motion and the fish out in the ocean
And the snow falling from the sky.
The lights go out round the swimming pool
There's a twister over the dunes,
The California girl is out there walking
In the shadows of a dead-eyed moon

The next morning while having breakfast I watched the burly motor bikers all sheepishly arrive for breakfast in their brand new gandoras, a kind of long nightshirt with shorter sleeves and no hood. They had presumably purchased them somewhere the night before on the streets and alleys of the town and agreed they should all wear them to breakfast. They looked like baby elephants in pyjamas.

And then, finally, we headed towards the old Glaoui fortress at Telouet. We were almost back at the starting point of our journey.

Getting there, Moha and I left the car and walked down a short slope to the Kasbah. After the burning heat of the desert back up in the mountains it was a grey, blustery, almost cool day. So this was it. It is hard for an Englishman to read below the surface of life in Morocco to what memories and feelings they have about those vicious times when Thami el Glaoui, with the backing of the French, could do almost as he wished

As I said before, Telouet did not really represent a kind of medieval past that had hung on into the 20th century. It seemed more an attempt to create one that had never really before existed.

Gavin Maxwell had visited only a very few years after the fall of the Glaoui, after Thami had attempted to depose the ruling Sultan as the French withdrew. The Moroccan people tired of his manipulation and intrigue and he fled to France to end his days in well-upholstered exile. The fortress on which a great fortune had been spent was abandoned and left to the ravens and the rats.

Even now, nearly sixty years later, Maxwell's words ring true.

Even in this setting the castle does not seem insignificant. It is neither beautiful nor gracious, but its sheer size, as if in competition with the scale of the mountains, compels attention as much as the fact that its pretension somehow falls short of the ridiculous. The castle, or kasbah, of Telouet is a tower of tragedy that leaves no room for laughter.

While visiting he persuaded a guard there to let him wander within and wrote:

It was on that night that, listening to the jackals howling, I became lost in the castle, and found my torch shining upon white but manacled bones in a dungeon. With the turbulent history of the Telouet they could have been either a hundred or less than five years old.

Now Gavin Maxwell was a dedicated storyteller, so how fanciful that was would be impossible to say, but it was easy to believe as Moha and I looked around.

Although you can visit it as a tourist destination, it feels half-hearted. It lies empty and echoing of ambition and greed. It is massive. Much of it remains intact, some of it apparently unexplored; fine mosaics and carvings sit alongside and within crude masonry and poor workmanship. It was never actually completed. Built in the mid 20th century it stands as a foolish vain folly to one man's arrogant attempt at immortality.

The sun reappeared as we left and as we drove back, Maha had one last surprise for me. Back in M'hamid I had wondered to him whether there was anyone still around who could remember the times when the Lords of the Atlas ruled.

He hadn't thought so, but said he would ask around. Somewhere down the road I was surprised to see Hassan, the mule boy, standing at the side of the road. He waved us to slow down and stop.

"I have found someone who worked for Thami al Glaoui," said Moha, looking quietly pleased with himself.

And then I noticed next to Hassan was a very short man in white traditional Berber dress. I got out of the car and went over and greeted Hassan and shook the little man's hand. When I say little, he was tiny - the top of his white hat reached just above my waist.

"Un nain," a dwarf, said Moha. "He comes from a village where there are many like him."

Once again it seems the mysterious is in plain sight, but we fail to see it. Was he a dwarf? I could not say because at one level of course they do not exist. They are characters from fairy tales, like goblins, or fairies. And nor was he presumably suffering from the genetic condition known as 'dwarfism'. For Moha had spoken of entire villages of these short people who are now intermarrying with the rest of the population and becoming lost in the flow of time.

The man was very reticent to talk to me through translation. The time of the Glaoui are still seen as bad times, explained Moha. People are still careful even though it was so long ago.

He suggested that it was better if he talked to him and then he would tell me later what was said. So I sat a little way away and attempted to chat with Hassan in French.

After we had we bidden farewell to Hassan and I had nodded respectfully and shook the hand of the former servant, Moha told me that the man had been a servant as a boy at Telouet. One of his jobs had been to climb up into the high mountains to collect snow and ice so that the warlord and his acolytes could have cold drinks all the year round.

The little man remembered hard times past, particularly under the rule of Thami's dreadful cousin Hamoud. Hamoud was as nasty a piece of work to his own people as he was to the world in general. He would take things from anyone and not pay for them. He forced the people of the village to work for free, building the kasbah and roads. Those who refused were punished with prison. People had to gather wood in far-off places in the mountains and cook couscous in their own homes and bring it to the Kasbah when the lord was entertaining.

Later, the little man worked in nearby salt mines and suffered greatly through times of starvation and fear. These days, though, life was better, and he said that the new King was slowly changing things.

And so, a hundred connections running around my head, we headed back to Marrakech. I had booked into a hotel on the outskirts, and we drove straight there.

Never did the overused phrase 'the sublime to the ridiculous' have more resonance. In fact, it was the sublime to the absurd. Three days previously I had sat in the desert under an acacia bush, dishevelled and disgusting but elated. My clothes walked home by themselves, but I was profoundly moved. I felt I had achieved something at the edge of my capability.

And now I was here. The psychological shock was a curious blend of funny and mournful. A first sight the hotel seemed one of those bland corporate palaces in which I have often stayed in the past. Everyone was very friendly and totally uninterested. I tested this by repeating the phrase "you know I've just walked 570 kilometres through the desert" to everyone I engaged with. Nobody reacted or even registered that information.

I was driven to my room in a buggy after saying a brief farewell to Ahmed and in particular to Moha. Moha, the ever patient, the determined, the curious and the tough. A friend.

It felt weird, as if I was stepping away from them into another world. It was as if I had to rush to say goodbye before we all simply melted away.

The hotel buggy drove me through large arches of manicured palm trees, past swimming pools where sparkling sapphire and amber lights made them glisten in the dark, to a large room where I was delivered and left.

I was disconcerted by the TV, the big double bed with white sheets, the whole white roses lying on the bed and little red rose petals strewn across it. At first, I couldn't move. I just stood there in my dirty Tilly hat, black T-shirt and scruffy shorts holding the backpack I had carried for over three weeks, not knowing what to do. Bizarrely my first move was to empty the contents of it into a pile. Heaven knows why. The GPS, the sunscreen, toilet paper, maps, my Leatherman, insect repellent, green and black Moleskine books, a compass, empty bottle of hand cleanser, Tuareg scarf, a jar of honey and a box of eating tools.

Then I sat on the end of the bed looking at the stuff and the wristband I had been given to wear. I turned on the television.

The first news of the Manchester bombings came through.

I havered on the portal between worlds.

Behind me stood Moha, the security police on motorcycles, the salt rivers, the cannon, camels and mules, the kindness of strangers, the weatherworn faces of Muhammad, Hassan and Zain, the high mountains and the endless desert.

And of course, Black.

Before me was home.

Roll of Honour

Thanks to all the people below who supported this book in its early stages.

Linet Arthur
Tansy Arthur
Nicky Ball
Jessica-Eve Bayliss
Nicola Brain
Benjamin Briggs
Sammy Carter
Judith Crosse
Matthew Crosse
Dr Bru Dahl-Meadows
Saskia Dahl-Meadows
Taz Dahl-Meadows
John Farquhar
Cilian Fennell
Orla Flynn
Greg Ford
Stephen Goldup

Peter Harvey
Stephen Johnson
Christopher Lydon
Mike McHugo
Ben McNutt
Dr Nigel Meadows
Nick Owen
Steven Pearson
Hugo Pound
Chris Shaw
Adam Snyder
Mary Thompson
Karen Trotman
Rob Twigger
Trevor White
Natalia Wieczorek